Too Easy

By Marcos Figueroa

Too Easy
By Marcos Figueroa

ISBN # 978-0-9986992-3-3

Edited by Eli Gonzalez and Lil Barcaski
Book Design by Ymmy Marketing LLC

For information address inquiries to:
www.aminutewithmarcos.com
or
www.theghostpublishing.com

Printed in USA

Foreword

My professional relationship with Marcos Figueroa began in 2010. I had recently been named President of a start-up insurance sales group, and we were gathering in Jamaica for our Annual Awards celebration. Marcos was a 2-year veteran of the company's sales organization and was to be honored as a top performer, for the previous sales year. I remember watching this young man as he "worked the room" shaking hands... meeting... greeting... and *learning* as much as he could from *anyone who was willing to talk*. It was apparent that Marcos possessed three key characteristics that are essential for success, determination, drive, and discipline.

Much of his drive and determination can be traced back to his youth and the time he spent serving our country as a U.S. Army Soldier. Marcos drew from the experience of his military deployment along with an insatiable desire to learn in order to formulate his personal approach to sales excellence. This system ultimately helped Marcos reach his potential as a sales professional. Today, you have the opportunity to utilize this same methodology and earn the income you desire.

This integrity-based sales system will help you - the reader, to attain higher levels of achievement by applying these straightforward principles of success. This book is predicated upon a fundamental understanding I came to realize at the beginning of my own career. We are not in the business of Selling... we are in the business of *Helping*.

I am convinced that anyone who follows the system Marcos outlines in his book and is willing to put in the necessary work can earn a six-figure income in the sales profession. Marcos has provided a plan - and if you work that plan, then you too will come to the realization that earning 100k a year or more in the sales profession really can be *Too Easy*.

Troy McQuagge
President & CEO
USHEALTH Advisors, L.L.C.
USHEALTH Group, Inc.

INTRODUCTION

Limitless opportunity. I'm surrounded by it. That's what fuels me. The more opportunity I have, the greater the impact I have on others.

My career is in sales, a profession that puts me in reach of countless possibilities, challenges, triumphs, and positive "life changing" outcomes. I'm in an industry where my income directly correlates with my commitment to excel, my skillset, and the value I provide to the marketplace. That's right, the more people I help – not sell, the more income I earn. In turn, the more income I earn, the more people I can help. Everyone wins!

If I can be candid here for a moment, one reason why I love being in sales is… I'm great at it, and I get to help more people as a result. There's nothing wrong with that. People should enjoy what they do so they might as well be great at it. I strive to be the best by staying committed and working effectively in conjunction with having great passion for servicing others. My income earnings over the years, compared to perhaps 97% of the other people in my industry, would solidify my straightforward declaration of being great at sales.

I enjoy the process of helping people. Within one call/meeting I can enroll them into a product that provides them considerable value. I often feel the sensation of fulfillment when I work because I know that if I do my job well and I do it ethically, other people are taken care of. After all, it means a lot when someone places their trust in me, ensuring that they end up in a better position than their current situation.

One of the main reasons why I love sales is because I've earned a substantial income in this field and continue to do so. To accomplish the goals I have set out for in my life, I need ample amounts of resources. Money is the primary resource. With vast amounts of income comes vast amounts of opportunity to help others. There are no monetary limits in my industry. That's what is so captivating about it! It's probably the main reason why you're reading this right now.

A sale, the exchange of a product or service for money, is the lifeblood of every business. In a world where many professions are in jeopardy of being replaced by technology and streamlined processes, such as manufacturing and skilled labor, it's reassuring to know that as long as I continue to improve and conquer the art of sales, I'll never be without a job or career. There has and always will be a demand for sales professionals who have mastered the craft of identifying with people and helping them find the solution to their problem. Not only will you always be in demand, but you'll also continue to make more money than most in your field.

I happen to work in the health insurance industry and find it exceedingly rewarding. I help provide benefits to protect individuals, families, and small businesses that will safeguard them from health or finance related disasters. Medical expenses have seemingly spiraled out of control, and access to the type of care people need has dwindled in the marketplace. One accident, one mildly lengthy hospital stay, one bad fall, can very easily cripple a family's finances. I help provide that security blanket for people and, because it gives them peace of mind regarding coverage and health, in turn, they can spend their energy and resources on enjoying their lives.

Not too long ago, I was on the phone with a small business owner that lives in the Tampa, Florida area. He did not have any health insurance and figured he should start shopping for coverage. I was determined to find a solution to his problem to help him avoid being exposed to financial ruin if anything catastrophic happened. I was relentless in my pursuit to help him – because I learned a long time ago that the most successful people on this planet are often the most persistent. He ended up signing on to one of the most comprehensive plans to which I had access. A few months passed, and I received a frantic phone call from his wife. She informed me that her husband had been in a serious motorcycle accident and wanted reassurance that their health plan would cover him and provide the protection he was going to need. She simply wanted to know that they would be all right.

My client was in the ICU for two weeks and lost one of his legs due to the accident. He was required to stay in the hospital for an extended period of time. He was a self-employed business owner and quite frankly, they weren't prepared financially or logistically to operate the business without him. When I pulled up the details of his health plan, I quickly called her back and put her mind at ease. "Everything will be fine, I promise."

Due to multiple operations requiring a lengthy hospital stay, his medical bills accumulated to slightly over 1 million dollars. The amount they had to pay - zero. In fact, because I placed him in a plan that covered what he may need one day and not based on a lower price to get the sale, he received a check for $30,000 for his dismemberment and an additional $20,000 from an accident benefit. It enabled him to use that money to pay his deductible and to hire the staff required to keep his business afloat while he recovered.

He professes his eternal gratitude to me to this day. He, his family, and his business are doing just fine even as he's on his second prosthetic since the accident. THAT is why I love what I do because I help people. THAT is why it's important for me to be great at what I do. THAT is why I won't get outworked. There's simply too much on the line for me personally, and for the people I can help.

I got my start in sales back in September of 1996. I initially started off in the mortgage industry and quickly learned that making a significant income wasn't just for highly paid Wall Street suits and medical professionals. It was in that industry that I was finally able to break into the six-figure income bracket. I then transitioned into the health insurance industry in 2009 after the market crash of 2008. I had to change what I was doing since I came from a market that was based more on "order taking" than it was on commitment and skillset. However, it wasn't until I returned from a combat tour in Afghanistan in 2014 where my mindset took a dramatic shift. I was deployed with my Army Reserve unit, and while I was there, I engaged in reading multiple books so I could become a better leader of Soldiers and to help keep my mind positive. It showed me the power of reading, and I brought my new habit back to the states and applied it to my civilian career. I was more motivated, more prepared, and more anxious to make an impact not only in my life but the lives of others.

In 2015, as a newly minted leader, I led my team to become the #2 sales team in our category in the entire company. A finely led and motivated team out of Nashville, TN edged us out for the top spot that year. We wanted to ensure that history wouldn't repeat itself in 2016. Later that next year, I drove to Nashville to shadow the top team and their leader **Doug Krull** to see what they were doing that we weren't. The biggest thing I took away from that visit was the fact that they were so willing to help even though they knew we wanted to surpass them. They gave us great ideas to take back with us and implement. We executed our plan, and by the end of the year, we were the #1 sales team for the company. It wasn't enough, however, to have the #1 team in the country. I prefer to lead from the front, and in doing so, I feel I must personally produce as well. With commitment, an absolute conviction in what I do, and a burning desire to be successful in sales, I was also recognized for personal production as well. As a leader of sales professionals, it is vitally important to show others that it is possible. Preparation and mindset were key.

I wrote this book for many reasons. I wanted to put my passion, mindset, and ideas on paper and share them with others. Over the course of my career, I've helped many people earn more money than they ever thought they would. I hope that by sharing what I know with you, it will change your thinking as well as your habits. If you're in sales but not earning at least six figures a year, you are still in amateur status and probably need to work on your commitment, your attitude, your mindset, and possibly even change your environment. Every single work day, you are presented with unborn opportunity. If you follow the strategies in this book, it will help you give birth to an entirely new way of life. You just need to be willing to give up your excuses and trade your poor people problems for rich people problems.

There are also many talented, engaging, influential people that don't work in sales but probably should. They're working in retail, in factories, or serving others in restaurants. Some may not have college degrees and feel that a professional sales job is only attainable through a four-year degree. Not true. I'm not some rich kid from Manhattan. I didn't go to the University of Michigan or an Ivy League school. In fact, I didn't go to college at all. I barely graduated high school! When I got out, my desire was to serve this country, and that's what I did. Now I have a new desire. To make a positive impact in this world and not be invisible.

My parents helped shape and mold me into the person I am today. That is why it's vitally important that you surround yourself with the right people. The U.S. Army provided me with the foundation of discipline and character. School couldn't teach me that, nor can it you. You don't have to pay tens of thousands of dollars to get a degree and then hope you get a job that pays you $50K a year. Not in America. This country offers limitless opportunities for those who believe what others don't and those that are willing to work for it.

If I had to narrow it down to one reason why I wrote this book, this is it: For some reason, in the minds of many people, the $100,000+ a year mark is an unachievable goal. I just wanted to chat with you. I wanted to have a candid conversation with you about... you. What do you want out of your life? What do you need to change? What do you need to improve?

Here's a truth many people can't fathom. It's much easier to earn six figures in 12 months in sales than people think. I'd like to share this truth with sales forces all over the country. I'd like to motivate good people and show them how easily it can be done with hard work, determination, and focus.

If you want to earn six figures a year, apply the principles I've carefully articulated in this book. If you do, you'll realize that I wasn't 100% honest with you. It's not easy to make six figures in sales - it's Too Easy.

TABLE OF CONTENTS

PREFACE

I grew up as a kid in Michigan just south of Detroit and followed sports religiously. Always rooting for the hometown Detroit Red Wings and Michigan Wolverines. Sports occupied a large amount of my interest and led me into playing soccer all through my childhood years. Cars were another fascination of mine since my dad worked for the Ford Motor Company and we lived in an area surrounded by automobile factories. Automobile manufacturing was one of the primary sources of employment in the Detroit area, so it was only natural to see Ford, GM, and Chrysler products all throughout the region.

At the age of 10, I moved to Ohio where the next 8 years shaped my future. Still heavily involved in soccer and my undying interest in cars, my focus was weak when it came to school. I knew at an early age that college was not my path. I began to have an interest in military service, and it was then that I enlisted at the age of 17 into the U.S. Army. 7 short months later after my 18th birthday, I shipped off to Ft. Knox, KY to start my basic and advanced initial training at the U.S. Army Armor School.

After training was complete I was then assigned to my first duty station at Ft. Carson, CO. I had never seen mountains like those in Colorado. That is when it hit me that there was so much to see not only in our country but all over the world. After my initial 4-year enlistment on Active Duty, I then transferred into the U.S. Army Reserve and started my civilian career in mortgage sales back in Cleveland, OH.

I was a loan officer with aspirations of earning $60,000 a year like my good friend Dell Reece who was also in the business. I thought $60,000 was a lot of money at the time. It was double what I earned in the military. A couple of short years after that I moved to Virginia Beach, VA and that is where my sales career took off at another mortgage company.

I surrounded myself with people who were earning well over six figures. The CEO of that mortgage company was well mannered, smart, committed to success and sharing it with others. He always took care of us and lived the life that I always wanted. Fast forward to 2009, after the market crash of 08,' I entered the health insurance industry as a licensed agent and found an organization with a dynamic culture built on high moral values and integrity. I knew this is where I needed to be. I knew this is where I could take the next step in further advancing my knowledge and skillset into the marketplace.

It was here that I began to **earn** the type of money I had always envisioned . I have made plenty of mistakes along the way, and I've gone through my share of hard knocks , but my losses became lessons, and my wins became constant.

I hope you're done making mistakes and are ready to **earn** money. Serious, life-changing money.

Chapter 1

MINDSET

In order for this book to shift your mindset in a way that provokes actions that will enable you to make more than six figures a year, you have to believe that you can. Belief is the most powerful motivator known to mankind. When you have absolute faith in your ability to accomplish a goal, the detractors and doubters in your life will be unable to penetrate your belief and you will succeed beyond measure.

When someone believes they can do something, they're halfway there. Before you go too far into this book, take a moment to assess your self-value, your talents, and your goals... and believe that you deserve to **earn** at least $100,000 in the next 12 months. Believe it; because the truth is, the world doesn't need just another sales book.

Belief is the most powerful motivator
known to mankind.
Marco-ism

Sales books are everywhere. There are millions of them. Just about every way to sell a product or service has been discussed, dissected, operated on, streamlined, taught, and viewed. And let's not forget the thousands of CD's, DVD's, Audio Books, Podcasts, and YouTube videos that coach, teach, and instruct on how to sell. The money-making secrets for sales people are out. Actually, they've been out for so long they are no longer secrets.

Still, millions of sales people have never made six-figures in a year. Is it really that difficult?

The truth? It's not easy, but it's not hard. Then again, whether something is easy or hard all depends on that person's abilities and commitment.

For a majority of salespeople, it's been more than hard, it's been impossible. A report on Foxbusiness.com stated that the average median household income in America across all jobs was $51,939 a year. The National Average Wage Index on the Social Security Administration website states that the average median household income in America was $48,098.

So, is **earning** more than $100,000 a year difficult? Based on those numbers, yes. Most people never make it. Less than 2% of Americans make $100K a year. But that doesn't mean it *has* to be hard.

If you ask sales people who earn more than $100,000 a year if it's difficult, they'll tell you that it wasn't as hard as they originally thought. I have been making much more than that for more than a decade. If you ask me, I'll give you the same answer I gave our commanding officer while I was deployed in Afghanistan when he would issue out our orders, "Too Easy."

Climbing a mountain is difficult, running 26 miles is difficult, dunking a basketball is difficult, juggling is difficult, and trigonometry is difficult for some. For others, those that have done it, over and over again, it's not hard at all, it's easy. For the professionals, it's easier than easy, it's too easy.

I've been able to earn a significant income over and over again, year after year. Along the way I have shown others how to do it as well. If you follow the guidance I've laid out in this book, you too could have the same success. All you need to have is the belief in yourself and the commitment to make it a reality.

What's Your Why?

First, I want you to ask yourself this one question. Why is **earning** six figures a year important to you?

Do you want to be the first person in your family to reach that milestone? Maybe it's because you want to be the first homeowner in your family? Are you tired of having poor people problems and want to trade them in for rich people problems? Do you want to become a person that others want to emulate and be a person who can give others hope? Maybe you want to send your kids to college or just make sure your kids have more than you had when you were growing up. Maybe you're single and think that more money will help you get the right partner. Whatever your reason is, it needs to be strong enough to carry you through the challenges you will face. Otherwise, you'll fail like so many others.

Your belief in yourself and your "why" is crucial to your success. If getting to $100,000 a year is a road trip, your *belief* is your compass and your *why* is your gas. Whatever your *why* is, own it.

> *"Your belief is your compass and your why is your gas"*
> **Marco-ism**

My Why

My *why* was my father. He's been a great dad all my life, and he always looked out for me. During my early adulthood, I couldn't seem to get on track. He was always there for me, providing me support… and by that, I mean he would help me with money. I always seemed to need financial support. There were times when I made really good money. However, I would somehow find a way to spend it foolishly. Luckily, my dad was always there for me just as he'd always been when I was growing up. He worked for the Ford Motor Company and picked up many double shifts, often working seven straight days a week for months on end.

My dad never made me feel bad about needing money. He always told me to ask him for help if I ever needed it, and he made sure he was close to me no matter where I lived so that he could help. When I moved to Virginia Beach my parents soon followed, wanting a change from the cold weather of northeast Ohio. My parents soon followed, wanting a change from the cold weather of northeast Ohio. Then, September 11th happened, and I was called to deploy with my unit. Upon my return from my deployment, I was transferred down to Tampa. As was previously the case, my parents followed me. My father knew that I may still need him, so it was important for him to be close to me. My dad had retired so only mom was working. There he was, looking out for me again, just in case. A few short years later my mom went to be with the Lord. Now it was just my dad there to help me when it should have been me taking care of him. Shortly after that, I vowed that I was going to change.

Hopefully, you're at the point where you're ready to make a change. I hope you're sick and tired of being sick and tired. I hope you're tired of not making enough money because there is no way you're going to create serious change in your life unless you're absolutely committed to it, the way I finally was.

I began to read sales and motivational books, at first just five minutes in the mornings. That soon turned to 10, 15, 30 minutes. I began to read at night. I was a sponge. I remembered reading that I needed to protect my thoughts and to think positively and the best way to do it was to shield myself from the negativity of the world. One evening, as I watched the News on television, I realized that I'd sat through twenty minutes of non-stop negativity. That was the last time I saw the News. I went from three televisions down to one which I keep upstairs in my media room so I don't pass by it as I walk throughout the house.

I began reading three books at a time, devouring knowledge. I couldn't let myself get in a situation where my father would have to bail me out again. I was desperate to change the trajectory of my life. I opened myself up to the wisdom of the sales greats like Zig Ziglar, Grant Cardone, Frank Bettger, Jeff Gitomer, Og Mandino, and Tom Hopkins. I started to let the coaching of self-help gurus like Tony Robbins penetrate my way of thinking. I had to change.

And change I did. In a year's time, I had turned my life around. I thought differently. I acted differently. I worked differently. And I expected differently. The result? I crushed the six-figure barrier, never to look back.

My father was able to move to Chicago so that he could be closer to my sister and his grandchildren. He was happy and confident knowing that I didn't need his financial support any longer. I was never so pleased and proud that due to the changes I made in my life, it made other people's lives better. He was my *why*, and I could bear any "*how*" it took to get there. Again, I ask you... what's yours?

How Bad Do You Want It?

You have to want to be successful in order to be successful. There's a great story about Socrates who was walking along the beach with his pupil, an eager and intelligent young man.

"Master, I've been with you many years, and although you've taught me so much, I still don't know the secret to being successful."

Socrates looked at the young man and said, "Follow me."

He walked into the ocean with the young man a step behind him. They walked into the water, chest deep. The young man was wondering why they were in the water when suddenly Socrates grabbed him and pulled him under. The young man didn't struggle, he held his breath, calmly wondering what insight his master wanted to teach him. As he began to run out of oxygen, he tapped his master's hand wanting to be let up. However, Socrates tightened his grip instead. Soon, the young man began to flail and push back against his master, fighting for his life, yet Socrates was a strong old man, and the young man stayed submerged.

The pupil struggled with all his might, realizing that if he didn't breathe soon, he would drown. Socrates let the young man go. He jumped up, taking in the deepest breaths he had ever taken in his life as his master walked to the shore.

A few minutes later, the student, utterly perplexed and visibly upset, reached the beach where his master stood.

"Why did you do that? Did I upset you?" The pupil asked, as calmly as he could.

"You wanted to know the secret to success, right?" Socrates asked.

"Yes, but…"

"When your head was under water, what was the one thing you wanted more than anything?"

"To breathe. I needed air."

Socrates began walking away, and his pupil caught up to him, still not realizing the lesson.

"When you desire to be successful, as badly as you needed to breathe, you will be successful."

People that desire success are willing to leave their comfort zones to get it. Comfort zones are traps preventing you from making a life instead of just making a living. Motivated people are willing to change their bed times, their circle of friends (if their "friends" hinder their chance for success), and even their diet. They envision a better life and realize that if they keep their old life alive, their new life will never materialize.

PLN A

That's what it says on my personalized U.S. Army license plate; it stands for Plan A. One of the things I learned from the many books, workshops, motivational seminars, and everything else I did to transform my life, is that you can't have a backup plan. Plan B is a dream killer. Back up plans are for people who aren't confident in what they are doing. They lack the conviction to see things through and make it work. They are already telling themselves it's ok if they don't make it because they can just go back to doing what they've always done.

Plan B is a dream killer.
Marco-ism

To change your life requires a commitment, and make no mistake about it, if you've never even made $40K, $50K or

$60K a year, once you earn $100K - it will change your life. Your level of commitment needs to transfer from the action of reading this book, into tangible changes in the way you work , and potentially , in the way you live . You 'll never benefit from what you know; you'll benefit from what you do. One thing I know for sure , if you 're not making six figures now and you keep doing things the same way, you'll never hit that magic number . And that number is just the start.

---

*You'll never benefit from what you know; you'll
benefit from what you do.*
Marco-ism

So, lose your back up plan. Lose your "if" – If this doesn't work out I can always _____. From here on out, commit yourself to changing your life, to making much more money than you ever have before, and to creating new success habits. Set your mind to thinking, *whatever this book tells me to do, I'm going to do it.* You owe it to yourself. You owe it to your "why."

Take an Action Step:

I'd like to challenge you to stop reading right now and gather your thoughts on what motivates you. Write down your *WHY.* Why are you reading this book? Why is making six figures important to you? Go ahead, write it down.

Now that you know your why, if it's authentic to your true self, you're ready for change.

Fortune favors the bold my friend. Be bold. Open your mind to the advice given in this book. If you let it, I promise you it will change your life.

Notes

Chapter 2

ACCOUNTABILITY

True Story

Detroit Tigers pitcher, Armando Galarraga, was well on his way to making history. It was the 9th inning, one out, and he was pitching a perfect game against the Cleveland Indians on June 2, 2010. The 27th batter he faced, Jason Donald, hit a grounder to the first basemen, forcing him away from the base. As is typical in this type of play, Galarraga sprinted towards the base, reached it, and caught the ball before Donald landed on it. On the telecast, the announcer called it an out before the umpire made his call.

The umpire's hands came across his chest, and he moved them out wide, "Safe!"

It was a home game for Detroit, so the crowd booed their displeasure. Tiger's player's and ownership had looks of disbelief, some with their hands on their heads. It was clearly an out. History was about to be made. But first base umpire, Jim Joyce, called Jason Donald safe. By the way, Donald was also surprised by the call.

After the game, Jim Joyce sought the replay. After seeing the play from a couple of different vantage points, he realized he had made the wrong call.

Here is where Accountability comes into play. Jim Joyce sought out Armando Galarraga and tearfully, man-to-man, apologized to him for making the wrong call. He then went to the media and acknowledged his mistake.

When Galarraga was asked about the wrong call by a reporter, most likely trying to exacerbate the issue and turn it into some sort of scandal, Galarraga said, "Nobody's perfect. I give the guy a lot of credit for admitting his mistake and apologizing to me." When they asked what else happened, Galarraga said, "I gave him a hug." The sportsmanship and class demonstrated by Galarraga and Joyce earned them widespread praise for the handling of the incident.

Joyce had owned up to his mistake to the world and apologized for costing a young man his rightful place in baseball immortality. I love it when people hold themselves accountable. When they aren't afraid to do the right thing even though it might not be the popular thing to do. Taking accountability for one's actions builds huge trust dividends. To me, being accountable means realizing that you are ultimately responsible for everything that impacts your life. I focus more on what happens because of me than what happens to me.

"Focus more on what happens because of you instead of what happens to you."
Marco-ism

Do You Know Your Best?

In this day and age, we are all too quick to blame others; the government, the weather, the traffic, the flat tire, the argument with the spouse, etc. If you're in sales, you might have heard struggling salespeople blame the leads, the market, or the price.

Failure and mediocrity have permeated our society to the point that when a child loses at something, the parent is supposed to say, "That's okay. You did your best." But did they? The child may not have practiced, opting to play video games instead, losing to people who did practice, but knowing they will hear that it's okay because they tried their best. Sorry, but that wasn't their best. They never actually reached their best because they weren't held accountable, by either themselves or their parents.

Participation trophies are handed out like Skittles, filling kids' heads with hollow accolades, like the sugar rush that fills their bodies, only to leave them nearly empty. I see a nation of people that settle for less: less effort, less energy, less knowledge, and yes, less money. I think to myself, *if they would just go that extra mile, get out of their comfort zone, commit themselves to live better lives personally, financially, and emotionally, how great could living in this country be?*

There's a difference between trying your best and doing your best. If you go to work unprepared and with the wrong mindset, even making more calls than ever before doesn't mean you tried your best. Trying your best takes preparation; holding yourself to a daily standard to be better than you were the day before. Millions of people, if they don't change, are destined to live their entire lives never knowing what their best is. But this is not about those people; this is about you. After all, you're the one investing your time in reading this book while your friends are watching TV or posting on Facebook.

Do you know what your best is? Can you honestly look at yourself in the mirror and truthfully tell yourself that you've done your best? Have you settled for "good enough" and never went all out for great? Has the perception of your reality, your limits, and your abilities, minimized your goals? If so, shouldn't you be upset with yourself?

Battle Buddy

Many people find the strength and resolve they need in an accountability partner. It's always easier to achieve something with someone else. The problem is, people either pick the wrong person or go about holding each other accountable the wrong way.

Selecting an accountability partner should not be predicated on who you get along with the best. Nor should it be a popularity contest. A great accountability partner would be someone who is where you want to be, someone who is doing what you are striving to do.

Part of my duties is to interview and offer an opportunity to the right people. Let me tell you, there are many great interviewees out there. In fact, I'm convinced that people prepare more to interview than when they actually get the job and have to go work. Everyone knows to say the right things in an interview; I'm a hard worker, I'm driven to succeed, I'm money-motivated, I'm dependable, I'm a team player, etc. I recently interviewed a woman who said all these things and more. I offered her the opportunity to join our team and she accepted. The day she was supposed to start, she didn't show up. She called me at around 10 am.

"I know I said I would be there today, but I want to think about it some more." She had worked for five employers in the past five years. "I promise you, once I commit, I'm 100% all in. I just need another week to think through my options. Can I give you my answer next week?"

"No."

I ripped up her resume. How could I trust her? She had given me her word when she accepted the position, and we agreed on a start date. She broke her word and our agreement. Honoring your word is a vital part of being successful, and I'll touch on that again a little further on in this chapter.

There are many who I contract that get right to work… but not on work, on making friends at work. Sure, we all want to be liked, I get that. But you don't go to work to make friends. You go to work to make money for you and your family. Forging friendships at work is a side bonus, not the goal.

Oddly enough, the ones who have time to chat with those new, uber-friendly associate types are people who are average earners. Soon, these newbies fall into bad habits and also become average sales people making an average or below average income. They don't bother trying to befriend the person who's at the top of the sales board in the organization. Maybe they think that person is "too serious" or "not approachable." The reality is, they're dead wrong. The top performers are almost always very approachable. He or she is just busy working most of the time. However, if during a break, you went up to that person and asked for help, he or she would help you. I have an idea: offer to buy lunch!

The best accountability partner, in most cases, is a top producer. Stroke that person's ego by asking him or her to teach you how to excel. If you ask the right way and stroke that person's ego right, you'll find the best accountability partner in that office.

That person may turn out to be your mentor. They've reached the heights you aspire to. They know the road map, the pitfalls, the right things to say and do, the right people and situations to avoid. The only thing you can learn from someone at the same level as you is where the bathroom is and how to use the software system.

When I first started working in the insurance industry, I chose a sales leader to be my accountability partner. I didn't want some average producer who thought he would probably to get fired every other month be the one teaching me anything. My good friend Jason Greif helped pave the way for me. He showed me how to start and run a successful sales office. He showed me how to attract the right people, how to select the right equipment, and how to effectively deal with different issues. Aided by his personal tutelage, I was able to show the people in my sales force how to **earn** six figures in their first twelve months.

The right accountability partner isn't going to accept your excuse for not doing what you said you were going to do. The right person won't let you slack. Instead, he or she will give you constructive feedback. The problem is that many in society are too weak to take any sort of criticism, even if it's to help them. Understand that a good accountability partner is there to help you, not enable you to fail and baby your ego.

Accountability

It's time for you to be accountable--to yourself. Don't lower the bar just because you tried and couldn't reach it. Go after it the next day, and the next. Go after it with a vengeance. Follow through with what you say you are going to do. If you make a plan to wake up at 5 am, read at 6, and be at the office fired up to go at 8 AM – do it. If one day you get to the office at 8:30, don't abandon your objective, get to the office at 8 AM the following day, and then the next, and the next. Grind it out and change your habits. Eventually, you'll hit your daily goals if you hold yourself accountable. You owe it to your self-esteem, your productivity, your future, your desired lifestyle, and your legacy to give one hundred percent. Any less would be selfish. It's not ok just to make enough money to cover your bills.

There's a book I love called *The Four Agreements* by Don Miguel Ruiz. It's been on the New York Times bestseller list for the last eight years. It's been translated into 40 languages worldwide with over six million copies sold in the U.S.; you might want to check it out. The four agreements are:

1. Be Impeccable with Your Word
2. Don't Take Anything Personally
3. Don't Make Assumptions
4. Always Do Your Best

I can go on and on, raving about that book; instead, I'm going to challenge you to get it and read it. Tell yourself right now, make a promise to yourself that you are going to read *The Four Agreements*. Be impeccable with your word and do it.

The main reason why I bring up *The Four Agreements* is because I'm on the topic of people who can't handle criticism. Mostly, any criticism towards you isn't even about you, it's more about the person saying it. Here's a quote from *The Four Agreements*:

Whatever happens around you, don't take it personally... if I see you on the street and say, 'Hey, you are so stupid,' without knowing you, it's not about you; it's about me. If you take it personally, then perhaps you believe you are stupid. Maybe you think to yourself, 'How does he know? Is he clairvoyant, or can everybody see how stupid I am?'

Mr. Ruiz is far from the only successful person to say don't take criticism to heart. Deepak Chopra claims to have a mantra he's said thousands of times:

I'm totally independent of the good or bad opinion of others.
I'm totally independent of the good or bad opinion of others.
I'm totally independent of the good or bad opinion of others.
I'm totally independent of the good or bad opinion of others.
I'm totally independent of the good or bad opinion of others.

Here's how to handle criticism: take it seriously, not personally.

If your accountability partner tells you that you're slacking and not living up to the agreement you made, don't take it as a personal attack. Don't get offended that he or she called you a slacker, take it seriously and stop slacking!

Take criticism seriously, not personally
Marco-ism

In order to get where you want to go, you can't fear resistance. Resistance isn't there to break you; it's there to make you. It's not the drive to the gym that makes your muscles grow; it's the resistance of the weight. It's not the shape of the sailboat that makes it move; it's the resistance between the wind and the sails. Without the resistance of water, a ship can't float. Without the resistance of air, those big Boeing 747's couldn't fly. Without the resistance of gravity, we wouldn't be able to walk across the ground. A rubber band is effective only when it is stretched. The tea kettle doesn't sing its song until it's up to its neck in hot water. Kites rise against the wind, not with it. If what you're doing doesn't have resistance, it's not worth doing.

When you decide to change your habits, you're going to get plenty of resistance. We tend to be creatures of habit, and the most resistance to change is going to come from ourselves. If you decide to get up an hour earlier, expect resistance from yourself. If you decide to eat healthier, expect resistance from your taste buds. If you decide to read motivational books during lunch, expect resistance from the social butterfly in you.

In the process of writing this book, I have experienced resistance. It doesn't always come in the same manner. I had committed to an every Friday appointment with the person helping me with this book. One particular Friday, everyone from the office was going out to lunch together, something that doesn't normally happen. I hadn't thought it through, so when I was asked if I wanted to go, I said yes. An hour before lunch,

I looked at my planner and remembered my standing Friday appointment. Being a believer in The Four Agreements and the First Agreement is to be Impeccable with Your Word, I did not feel good telling my work mates that I couldn't make it (resistance). However, I had made a promise to myself to write this book and to the person helping me, to meet with him on Fridays, so I went to my appointment and we worked on this book.

Resistance to your dreams has many faces. Sometimes it is blatant, and other times it is wily or guile. The thing to know about resistance is when you learn how to harness it to work in your favor, you can do big things. A river's force downstream can be harnessed to provide light and electricity to an entire city. You need to have a strong sense of accountability to resist the temptations that keep you from your goals. One of the biggest challenges you will face is normalcy. When you disrupt your behavioral pattern, you go against the very life you have created, your normal routine. In order to create a new normal for yourself, you need discipline.

Discipline

The backbone of accountability in the military is discipline. Military personnel understand their tasks. The message they receive about what they are expected to do is loud and clear. The word discipline has been typecast, like an actor who only gets cast to play a certain type of role. Discipline's connotation can stand for punishment or correction. And yes, those are correct definitions of what the word means. People in the military understand the repercussions of what will happen to them if they fail to do what they've been tasked to do. That knowledge of being disciplined is a major reason why many service personnel get their jobs done, whether they like it or not.

However, discipline also means self-restraint and self-control. That's the type of discipline needed for you to change your daily habits at home and at work in order to reach your monetary goals. It's all fine and dandy for you to make a plan, maybe even hang up a vision board that contains all of your short-term and long term goals, but if you don't have the self-control and discipline to follow through on them, the only thing you've achieved is to put two holes in the wall from the nails that your vision board hinges on.

In the military, accountability is everything. Service members die without it. Our country would be at risk if our service men and women weren't accountable to their oath. We would not have a system that works or a functional plan of attack to protect our country's citizens against enemies, both foreign and domestic. The only way to win a war or maintain peace is through discipline and accountability. A war is usually won after a series of difficult battles. Peace can only be attained through consistent effort.

If you've always wanted to make over six figures a year but never have, you haven't lost the war, but year after year you've lost battle after battle. It's time for a new battle strategy. As you continue to read this book, write down the strategy contained herein. Then, find an accountability partner, your battle buddy, a person that is financially where you want to be.

Your best requires Preparation.

Execution of a plan requires discipline.

Discipline is policed by accountability.

Accountability is the cornerstone of success.

Take an Action Step:

Select an accountability partner. Write his or her name here: _____

Let your accountability partner know what you would like from him or her and enter into a verbal or written agreement with that person.

Notes

Chapter 3

CREATE YOUR FUTURE

It's time to talk about your need for goals. You might not know it, but as hard as you may have tried, if you didn't have set goals, you've never even entered the game of accruing wealth. Why didn't you have crystallized, clear goals? Was it the day-to-day distractions that kept you from focusing on them? Maybe no one ever taught you the benefits of visualizing goals, writing them down, setting up a plan to achieve them, and then executing that plan. If you don't set goals for yourself, it's impossible to reach them. It's imperative to have a vision for where you want to be and what you want to accomplish on the way. On a road trip, if you have no destination how will you know when you've arrived?

If you used to set goals but don't anymore, somewhere along the road you've convinced yourself that you're not "goal-oriented;" that goals aren't a priority of yours. That may be why you're reading this book now; you've had an "ah ha" moment, and now you want a jump-start to get back on that road. You're tired of just existing, and you truly do *want* to excel. Welcome back to making a life, and not just living one.

The right goals are always hard to achieve, and they should be; but not out of reach. If you never feel like giving up, then your goals are too small. In other words, if you're not feeling the pain of making adjustments in your life, then you're not changing what you have always done. Reaching a goal *is* hard. It makes your life difficult at times, but, in order to get better at anything, you need to learn to embrace the grind, or as we said when my battalion deployed to Afghanistan, "embrace the suck." We knew that what we'd be asked to do was going to be difficult (that's the suck part), but completing the mission (goal) was well worth the sacrifice.

Now let's talk about the process of goal-setting. My first tip? Write out your goals and be specific. For example, don't write a goal like this: *I want to make a lot of money.* That's too vague. What exactly is a lot of money? If your goal is a new car, what type of car do you want? For many people, a used car they recently bought is a "new" car. So, do you want a new car or a used car that's new to you? Also, what type of car do you want? Is your goal to run your own home-based business or to grow your home-based business to a national sales force of 150 people generating an income of $10 million a month?

You are writing down your mind-set, and the mind is a powerful thing. There's a popular movie called *The Secret*, based on a best-selling book of the same title written by Rhonda Byrne in 2006. Basically, the actual "secret" is derived from the law of attraction. The book states that as we think and feel, a corresponding frequency is sent out to the universe, which attracts back to us events and circumstances on the same frequency. For example, when a person thinks/transmits happy thoughts into the universe, the person will attract that which gives him/her happiness. So if a person wants a new car and thinks positively about it, talks to people about it, test drives it, designates a parking space for it, and visualizes owning it, the law of attraction is set in motion making it likely that car is on its way.

I don't claim to have leveraged *The Secret* to my advantage, nor do I adhere to it wholeheartedly. But many do. To me, either in the book or movie, the message of *The Secret* is another form of goal setting. I do believe that when you put your mind to something, whatever goal it is, and put a realistic plan into action to achieve that goal, you have a great shot at obtaining it.

Be Specific

If your goal is to buy a Ferrari 488 GTB and you buy it, have you met your goal? Of course, right? Maybe not. If you mortgaged your house or it caused a divorce, or you can't make the payments, you really didn't reach your goal because now you can't afford it. There's a difference between setting a goal to get that car and getting that car while still being able to live comfortably.

Beware of the goals you set. If they are not well thought out and specific, reaching them can cause more harm than good. If you want to buy an $80,000 car, you better be prepared to comfortably handle all your financial obligations as well as any unforeseen expenses. And let's not forget to ensure that we're paying ourselves first by putting away money for retirement if that is a goal as well.

Case in point: I'm a big "car guy." Being that I was raised in the Detroit area I was naturally surrounded by the "Big Three" auto manufacturers. I grew up around cars and my friends were all into them. I always wanted a Porsche 911 but never thought it would be a reality. In 2007 I bought my first new Porsche. Setting aside money for a down payment was my first goal and I did that. However, I was living paycheck to paycheck. I put the $13,000 down that I had saved and got the car, but making the payments became stressful later on. My goal was shortsighted, and I paid for it in more ways than one. I failed to realize that I wasn't financially comfortable enough after achieving that goal. But I learned... the hard way. I had to sell the car among other things because I wasn't the right person at the time to get myself to the next level.

Fast forward 10 years, now I was the right person and able to order my next 911. It went for well north of six figures, but this time I was financially secure. At this point in my life, I could have paid cash but opted to put a large amount down and invest the rest. If I lose my source of income tomorrow, I'll still be able to make the payments and not worry about my finances. I'm not saying this to brag; I'm saying this to let you know that by making the right adjustments in your life you will be able to achieve similar success or greater.

Reaching your goals shouldn't hurt other areas of your life. Why buy your dream six-bedroom house if you have a family you need to support and the mortgage and insurance payments are going to keep you awake at night? Set the types of goals that are going to push you forward, not push you over a cliff.

Goal Book

I have a Goal Book. You should get one too. I write down every specific goal I'm shooting for. I include the details of every goal, while at the same time envisioning if I truly want to achieve it. (There have been times when I started out with a goal only to scratch it off once I've thought it through). Then I create a timeline to reach the goal. You may not always achieve them by your suspense date, but that's ok. It's still a goal you want to achieve. It's just might take a little more time and probably a lot more effort on your part. If there is a dollar amount to it, I add that as well. If it's a personal goal, like weight-loss, I get very specific with where I want to be at several points along the timeline toward my ideal weight.

Once I commit to a goal, I rarely change it, but at times I'll change the timeline. I'm not opposed to you changing your goals so long as your perspectives have changed. For example, if your goal is to buy a second home but you opt to buy a commercial property instead, that's still a goal. All you did was change the objective. However, I've never liked hearing about people who change a goal because it's too hard. Listen, life happens and gets in the way of goals, and we don't always get things when and how we want. That's why I will change the timeline rather than the goal. To change my well-thought out, desired, goal because it was harder than I thought, is akin to giving up. Don't set your bar lower, train harder and longer. If anything, set the bar higher. And even higher than that!

Unsuccessful people either don't set goals or set easily attainable goals. Some people's *goals* are so small that if they did nothing different, they would achieve them. They may call it a goal but it's not; time is a factor here. Goals are something that you reach by stepping out of your comfort zone and/or changing your habits.

The most successful people have the most ambitious goals. They know that if they hold themselves accountable for how they spend their time, money, and talent, they get closer and closer to reaching their goal. These are the types of people that are too busy to binge watch the entire series of The Walking Dead in a few days. They put a value on their time. Even their down time helps prepare them to reach their goals; down time energizes them, and when they get back at it, they are rested and ready. They're typically not spending their lunch hour going through Facebook and sharing funny cat videos. Instead, they're on LinkedIn, making key connections to get them closer to where they need to be or watching a video on how to become a multiplier and not a divider.

I encourage you to have big goals in arenas other than hitting that "six figure" a year mark. Visualize your dream life and start developing the blue print to build it. Be well rounded with your goals, don't make everything about money. Don't love money. Love what money allows you to do. Have spiritual, physical, and philanthropic goals as well.

Don't love money. Love what money
allows you to do.
Marco-ism

Tell others about your goals. Some people get embarrassed, thinking that perhaps others will poke fun at them if they knew their plans. Remember what you read in Chapter 2 about the Four Agreements? You are totally independent of the good or bad opinion of others. Instead of making your goals a secret, tell as many people as possible. Share them on social media. Post something like this:

By September of next year, I will be the proud owner of a Ford Mustang Shelby GT350 ($55K), and it won't break me. I'll be able to make the payments AND go out to eat whenever, wherever I want. If you consider me a friend, please hold me accountable.

What do you think that will do for your resolve to work smart and hard enough to reach a goal? Because you put a deadline on it – September of the following year – people will start asking by July if you're on track. When the day arrives to take delivery of that GT350, make a video of yourself getting in it. Share that on FB Live.

When you share your goals and speak confidently about your plans to reach them, it empowers you. Sure, some won't think you can do it. Let that fuel you, not break your spirit. Many will believe in you. Those that don't probably never reached any of their own goals. Don't be afraid to be an inspiration to others. Tenacity and determination are contagious. Start a revolution in your own circle of friends and family. Be the first to set the example.

Planning and Execution

Once you've established some clear goals, the next step is to figure out how you're going to reach them. To make life-changing money, you need to have the discipline to exercise life-changing habits. No part of your day should be unaccountable. Without discipline, your plan will not succeed.

My friend Eli is a big believer in life coaching. Some people feel they need it; some don't. But Joshua's life coach did an interesting exercise with him that I want to share with you.

"What are the four most important things you care about, Eli?" asked the life coach.

"My faith, my family, earning a great living for us, and my health," Eli replied.

Later in the session, the life coach gave him an excel spreadsheet that accounted for every half hour of the week. "I want you to write down everything you do in these half hour slots. I want a visual of your life so that we can see what adjustments might make sense."

The following week, Eli, ever the good student, showed his life coach what he did for seven days, one half hour at a time.

"Why did you lie to me?" the life coach asked.

"What do you mean?"

"Well, you said the four most important things to you were your faith, your family, your job, and your health. But looking at how you spent your week, it was all a lie. Watching television seems to be more important to you than all those things."

Eli's life coach went on to show him that while he went to church on Sunday, he never had prayer time or Bible study time. He had not set aside any quality time with his wife or children. He never put in any preparation time for work. And he went to the gym twice but went out to eat at fast-food restaurants four times.

He then asked Eli to *plan* the coming week by half hour segments and to intentionally add time for what he thought were the most important things to him. So Eli put in time to be home when his daughter got home from school three times a week. He put in time to shoot hoops with his son and to play video games with him. He put in time to go to a nice restaurant, just him and his wife. And he put in time to be alone and focus on his faith. He called it, *My Ideal Week.*

Today, Eli is a changed man, and although he doesn't live up to his ideal week every week, you can tell what's most important to him by where he spends his time.

What if you did that exercise? What would people say is most important to you based on how you lived your life last week? It's time to stop living average, don't you think? Set aside time to read, learn, dial, study, play, exercise, call your mom (she'd probably first yell at you for taking so long to call but after that your conversation will get better), and live the life you want, not the life you've been living.

Planning is so important because it narrows your focus and frees up mental energy for executing that plan and future plans. Many times when we get distracted, we don't realize it--because we're distracted! But if you have a plan for what you're going to do when you wake up, when you get to work, what to do after lunch, and what to do when you go home, distractions will find it nearly impossible to go undetected. Stay away from the time wasters. You always have to ask yourself, "is what I'm doing right now getting me closer to my goal?"

For me, my plan starts in the morning. Many people say they're not morning people. That can be changed. Perhaps you need to re-evaluate your friendships and see if they align with you reaching your goals or are holding you back from your goals. Maybe you drink a little too much every night and have a tough time clearing the cobwebs in the morning. Maybe you don't have the discipline to actually go to bed an hour or two earlier. Night owls can turn into early birds if they want to badly enough, and if it's part of their plan.

I wake up at 5:40 a.m. every weekday. I set out my clothes the night before so, in the morning, I'm not pressed for time. On days when I go to the gym, I pack my gym clothes in a bag and make sure I have everything I need for my workout and the shower after. After I hit that snooze button once and get out of bed, all I have to do is brush my tooth (I always say tooth, but I do have teeth), take a shower, get dressed, and head out the door.

I'm at a Starbucks every workday at 6:35 a.m. The caffeine jolts my body awake, and a great book gets my mindset on the right track. After 30 minutes of reading, I head over to the office to get in early. I never hit traffic on the way in because there is none. I make sure I get to a Starbucks right down the street. Look, we all have two options:

1. Go to bed a little earlier and wake up early to avoid traffic and feed your mind positive information and new ideas.

2. Sleep in a little longer and sit in traffic an extra 30 minutes every single workday. (Which translates to losing 2 ½ hours every week, which translates to losing 130 hours a year -5 ½ days - wasted, sitting in traffic in the mornings).

Which one gets you closer to your goals?

Once I'm at the office, I begin my workday in a fashion that's going to enable me to reach my goals. You know why I do this? Because I have a high self-worth. I deserve a better than average life, and I'm willing to go after it. I earn what I receive every day.

When I start dialing prospects, they're not talking to someone who is mundanely trying to reach a daily dial count; they're on the phone with a motivated, caring, educated, and skilled sales professional… and they don't stand a chance.

Want to know what I say to them? Flip the page…

Notes

Chapter 4

PROSPECTING

What are you afraid of?

We're all afraid of something. On the website, www.fearof.net, they list the top 100 phobias and fears. You might find some of yours listed here.

The top ten are:

1. Arachnophobia – fear of spiders
2. Ophidiophobia – fear of snakes
3. Acrophobia – fear of heights
4. Agoraphobia – fear of open or crowded spaces
5. Cynophobia – fear of dogs (from Poodles to Great Danes)
6. Astraphobia – fear of thunder/lightning
7. Claustrophobia – fear of small places
8. Mysophobia – fear of germs
9. Aerophobia – fear of flying
10. Trypophobia – fear of holes

Honorable mentions are #12 – Thanatophobia - fear of death, #13 – Glossophobia – fear of public speaking, and # 20 Trypanophobia – fear of needles. I find it odd that there are 11 fears higher on the list than dying but hey, I wasn't consulted when they developed the list.

While it interests me, and hopefully you too, to see what scares the living daylights out of most people, I have yet to find a Fears List for sales people. I believe that the top 3, from number 3 to number 1 would be:

3. Doing a presentation – fear of public speaking

2. Close – fear of asking for the money

1. Cold calling – dialing total strangers in hopes of selling them on a service or product.

(Before you get into this section I want to make it clear that there are "authorized" calls and texts and "unauthorized" ones. Make sure to abide by the National Do Not Call list.)

Cold Calling someone you do not personally know in advance, whether through "walking and talking" or by an authorized phone call, is for the strong minded, thick skinned, sales professional. It's no joke. It breaks more salespeople than anything else. However, it's interesting to note that cold calling is only a portion of what makes up Prospecting.

The problem with prospecting is that most people simply don't know how. Walking a tight rope scares me, however, those that have been trained at it and perfected it actually tight rope without a net underneath them. In the same way, I believe it can be argued that a fear of something could simply be because people have little to no experience with it, or know enough about it. So, let's get to know prospecting and see if we can't reason the fear out of you.

Prospecting for Potential Clients

Many people feel as if they have to adhere to a 9 AM to 6 PM time frame to do business. People with the mindset to help and serve, don't bother with those types of limitations. At times, I'll send texts early in the morning while I'm having my morning iced tea, regardless of the time zone of the other person. Why? Off-work hours are times when you're not competing against other salespeople; you're competing against shaving or make-up time. You now have the most important resource they have, their attention. Our phones are never far from us.

Phone texting plays a vital part in today's sales arena. Some people won't utilize this method of communication because they feel it's impersonal. I don't think they could be further from the truth. Texting is acceptable and expected with people who are comfortable with texts. It allows them to skip through pleasantries (fluff) and gets directly to the point. Many people enjoy that aspect of using text message. Put yourself in their shoes and ask yourself; would you rather take time listening to a long-winded voicemail or would a short text get your attention making it easier to reply? This tactic breaks down barriers between sales people and their prospects. Psychologically, the prospect unwittingly puts you in the friend zone, since those are the people he or she normally texts. I text early – amateur sales people aren't working that early.

It is far more likely that your text will be answered than your voice mail will. In the 45 seconds it takes to dial, wait for the greeting, and leave a voicemail, you could have dialed more prospects and sent several more texts, or more importantly, actually talked to a live person who picked up your call!

Your text will be answered more often than your voicemail
Marco-ism

Don't both dial and send a text. If you want to do both at the same time, get a dialing system that automatically sends out text when dialing that number. Either get in a groove of dialing or sending out texts but don't try to switch between the two. It's all about rhythm. Get into a rhythm and run with it. The end goal is to reach a live voice on the other line. Making calls will get you there quicker. Save the texting for later when you're on a short break.

I once had a new hire shadow me while I made calls to authorized numbers. He had worked in sales for over fifteen years but had an unremarkable career up to that point. I made the first dial, and the person didn't pick up. When the greeting came on, I hung up. Five seconds later, I called the same person again. When the greeting came on, I hung up. Five seconds later I called again. When the greeting came on, I hung up and dialed someone else.

"Why did you call the same number three times in a row? Wouldn't it be more effective to leave a voicemail and move on? You could have reached three people in that same time frame."

That logic makes sense to some people... but most don't make six figures.

I looked squarely at him.

"I'm most effective when I talk to people on the phone. When I call three times in a row, out of curiosity, if nothing else, people will answer. They may think it's a friend or relative calling from another phone due to a dead phone battery. It could be a service provider that was going to call them back about a request they put in. The bottom line is that they rarely answer voicemails."

He wasn't convinced. By the time we took a ten-minute break that afternoon, I had spoken to more people in one day than he ever had before. I had done that without calling nearly as many people as he called. Even those people who didn't pick up after my third ring will inevitably call back when they get a free moment.

If you use the phone to make dials in your sales , connections with live people must be the goal , not the number of dials. I'm not saying the number of dials is not important, not at all. I believe in outworking my competition. I am saying that getting to your prospects is your first goal.

If you made 100 calls in a day by calling on only 100 people and left voicemails when someone didn't answer, you might have left 90 voicemails and talked to 10 people.

If you used my method of hanging up and calling back twice before leaving a message, you might have made 200 calls, left 60 voicemails, and talked to 40 people. If you quadruple the number of people you talk to, what's the likelihood that you could quadruple your sales?

There's a great book I read called, *Go for No! Yes is the Destination, No is How You Get There,* by Richard Fenton. In it, he shares what it takes to outperform 92% of the world's sales people. It's a great read. Richard goes deep into what failure is and isn't, and how to get past it. Much of what he wrote in his book has been directly or indirectly transposed into this one. His words helped change the way I view the workday, as I hope my words do for you.

I use a dial sheet so I can see how many calls it takes to get a hold of someone. The numbers don't lie unless you cheat yourself by not filling out the sheet. In order for me to make the type of money I need to make, I don't make 10 calls and take a break. Not me. I'm laser focused on my annual earnings. I reward myself based on activity. I'll take a Starbucks (iced tea) break ONLY after 150 calls.

Killer Breaks

Breaks are necessary but they can also turn into lengthy distractions. It's the time you talk to coworkers or get pulled in different directions which interrupts your flow. Distractions are Wealth-Building-Killers. Taking **too many** breaks **can** break you! They keep you from getting to a person on the other end of the phone that needs your service . They stop you from getting where you want to go. Make it a point to guard your attention. It's your most valuable resource and is one that many others squander.

Some sales people love to take long social breaks. They see someone get up from their cubicle, and a moment later, they're standing next to him or her. Soon, they're laughing, drawing attention to themselves, and having a good old time. Now, I love to laugh and enjoy myself as much as the next person, but I laugh louder and enjoy myself more when I reach my monetary goals, and I'm able to do special things with the people I love.

This is the mindset it takes to make more money than ever before in your life. Nothing worth having comes without sacrifice. We've all heard that before, but do we really take in what it means or how it affects our outcomes? I encourage you to sacrifice being the most liked person in the office, the funniest person in the office, the office shrink, the office YouTube video watcher, the office mom, the office sports professional, the office community builder, and the office hard ass – and focus on productive work during work hours. I promise you it will pay huge dividends.

Nothing worth having comes without sacrifice
Marco-ism

Posturing

In order to prospect at a high level, mind your posture. I'm not just referring in the physical way you stand, sit, or how you move your hands. Posture to me goes deeper. It has to do with confidence. Take the words, *maybe, perhaps, I think, I heard,* and other weak words out of your vocabulary. Once a person trusts the expertise of an individual and believes the individual wants to help, they are ready to be told what to do.

"OK, so here's what's going to happen next. Get out your credit card..."

That is posturing with confidence.

"No, I'm unable to meet for our networking meeting at 10 AM because I'll be making calls, but 7 AM works better and here's why; we'll still beat the morning rush, we can eat a good breakfast, and still have the entire day left without interrupting our work flow. I know a place with great coffee..."

Understand that you're always closing. The close isn't just sealing the deal. A great salesperson understands that there are several levels of a sales process and nothing starts without first getting the prospects undivided attention. So, in order to get the close you either need to start with an appointment or prepare for the "one call" close.

Some sales people prefer to use phone scripts while others don't. For those who don't know what one is, it's a written dialog on how to guide a prospect through a sales call or sales cycle and I highly recommend using one. It will guide you where you need your prospect to go.

Notes

Chapter 5

LISTS AND GROUPS

Leads Lists

If you can scrape up $100 to buy leads of individuals who have provided consent for you to contact them telephonically, do it. Investing in yourself means more than just reading good sales books. Talking to people beats not talking to people, all day, every day. If they're old consent leads, still buy them! Start looking at those old leads as (G)old leads. Think about it. Older consent leads contain prospects who have had life changing events. They may have gotten married, lost a job, moved, had a baby, and so on. (G)old leads are a great way to practice your closing techniques, and better yet, older consent leads are even cheaper to purchase!

Ashley McKee, a lead and top personal producer, swears old leads are gold leads. At one point in time those people were interested in our products but maybe a rookie messed up the sale. She has a script that works well for her. Here is a sample:

"It appears that a while back you were looking for information on xyz, did you ever get that taken care of?" or "I have a note that you wanted me to reach back out to you around this time and wanted to let you know there are new products available in your area."

That's a better start than, "Hello, is this Mr. Smith? Phillip Smith? Hi, Mr. Smith, this is John Doe, I'm calling from XYZ Company. How are you doing today?"

If walk-ins don't buy but leave their information, call them. They didn't come in just to blow some extra time they had left over. Skippy the new guy or Mary the drama queen, probably blew it. Wherever you're working, try to get a list of previous clients or one-time prospects that never bought. I remember getting lists like those and hearing co-workers say, "I called those people, they won't buy. They just weren't interested." The truth was, the salesperson just wasn't interesting.

I never said it out loud, but in my head, I thought, "Ya, but you're not me."

That is another example of posturing. I know that, because of my work ethic, preparation time, and conviction in what I'm selling, great things are going to happen. They already have! Believe the same. You might be the only person in your office reading a book on how to earn six figures. Once you apply what you learn here, which is getting up early, making the most out of your day by preparing for every conversation, and are obsessed with helping as many people as possible, you are going to make undeniable strides in both your career and your life.

Networking Groups

Networking groups are all the rage these days. If you've never been to one, allow me to enlighten you on what they are. Many people, mostly sales professionals and entrepreneurs, have assigned times when they meet with the same group of professionals to network. The groups that I'm aware of either meet in the late morning (10 am) for breakfast or during lunchtime. I belonged to a networking group that met weekly at 7 AM. I had relationships with strategic partners in the group, and when we would meet throughout the week, it would also be at 7 AM. We would have breakfast, discuss what we needed to discuss, and still have the entire day left. Whenever we couldn't meet in the morning, we would meet during lunchtime. Why? Because people that could use the service I'm selling are available to take my calls between breakfast and lunch or between lunch and dinner. Successful sales people don't make "busy" appointments. They make "necessary" appointments and plan those around "selling time."

In every networking group meeting, each member has the opportunity to promote his/her business for either 30 seconds or a minute, depending on the size of the group. Every few months one or two members get to advertise their business and themselves to the group for 10 or 15 minutes, again, depending on the size of the group.

The goal of the networking group is not necessarily to sell to the other members, although it happens often. It's to get the other members to trust you enough that they refer their circle of friends to you; people that you would otherwise never know. In essence, by maintaining a weekly presence with the same people, fostering trust along the way, each member becomes a quasi-salesperson for you. So, if you are in a group with 22 other people and they all trust you, you just gained 22 salespeople with access to hundreds of people.

Unfortunately, many professionals don't quite know how to "work" a networking group, and they end up creating distrust by trying to sell members of the group and by being selfish; meaning only taking referrals, but never giving any. Here's the deal, in any sales capacity you would be much more successful if you are selfless, not selfish. What you give, you will always gain, and then some.

Referrals are incredibly powerful. When you get a referral, the person being referred to you is almost sold. A trusted friend or family member has told them what a great person you are and how you will be fair, professional, and knowledgeable enough to help them get what they need. The referral is typically in the market, has the means to pay for the product/service you can provide, and in most cases, feels that if he or she doesn't go with you, they will let down the mutual friend you share. There is no reason why your closing ratio should be less than 90% from a solid referral. None. That's the power of networking groups.

I'm a believer in networking groups, so long as your primary focus is to provide referrals to others. The psychology of a good person is to reiterate when a good thing has been done for him or her. Let's suppose you're in a networking group and the real estate agent of the group handed you five referrals in five weeks. Would you not want to thank her by giving her a referral? The next time you hear people talk about buying or selling their home, wouldn't you bring up that real estate agent? Of course, you would. That's the secret of success for networking groups, being selfless, not selfish.

Networking Events

These events are different than networking groups, so, your strategy needs to be different. A networking event could attract anywhere from 30 to 200 people, sometimes more. Typically, these events are centered on a particular theme and bolstered by invited speakers. Before, in between, and after the presenters speak, there is usually time to network. Here is where many people fail.

They go to these events with a pocket or pocketbook full of cards and gear up to work the room. During the networking time, they meet as many people as they can and one by one they give them their business cards. They go home happy that they've given away 30 business cards and wait for the phone to ring... and wait... and wait. Some people are probably still waiting for one of the people they met at a networking event to call them. No one is going to call. They already used the back of your business card for a reminder note. They were all about themselves, and no one likes to work with selfish people.

No one likes to work with selfish people
Marco-ism

Back in June of 2011, I was at an event that changed my life. It was a fundraiser for the Wounded Warrior program being held at the VA hospital in Tampa, FL. There were over 20 wounded warriors of the Iraq and Afghanistan wars along with their families who stayed in town during their recovery. The first, and what turned out to be the only wounded warrior I met, was Sergeant First Class Cory Remsburg, a U.S. Army Ranger with the 75th Ranger BN who was wounded by an IED (improvised explosive device) during a routine patrol in Kandahar, Afghanistan in 2009. He was blown back by the blast that took a large chunk of his skull as he fell face down in a pool of water. He was in a coma for months while his mother and father were by his side. I spent most of my time talking with his mother since Cory had challenges with speech. I saw firsthand what the donations to these programs do for Soldiers like Cory. Had it not been for my sincere desire to learn as much about him as possible, I may never have had my photo taken with the Soldier who was later honored at the 2014 State of the Union address. There he was, honored by President Obama while standing with his father to his right and First Lady Michelle Obama to his left. That visit left such a lasting impact on my life that it inspired me to reenlist back into the U.S. Army Reserve in July 2011. Two short years later, I would find myself deployed to the same country as SFC Remsburg found himself just 4 years earlier. If I did what most others would do, shaking hands with as many people as possible and saying thanks, I may never have had that opportunity to meet someone that literally inspired me and changed my life.

Take the time to be present in your conversations. Get to know the person, not just what they do. We all love to talk about ourselves, so, ask them questions. Don't just ask the same boring business questions; ask them about their family, sports, foods they like. If they ask about you, answer them and then direct your attention right back to them.

Here is a sample of my side of a conversation at a networking event, once we've told each other our names and what we do:

Are you married?

Any children?

Oh really, that's great. How old?

So, how long have you been living in this area?

I'm from Chicago myself, not a fan of the cold though, and I don't think I'll ever go back. Are you originally from a cold state?

Wyoming? I think you're the first person I've ever met from Wyoming. What part?

I've never heard of it, is that a rural area?

What caused you to move from there? Oh, your career?

You seem very passionate about what you do. What is it that makes it tick for you?

Where does most of your business come from?

I'm not sure if you can see it, but I'm selling my butt off. I'm not talking about my product, I'm not talking about my service, I'm not qualifying, I'm not trying to gear the conversation to me, I'm not rushing the conversation, and I'm not talking pricing, – but I'm selling!

As you can see, before our conversation ends, I'll circle back to what that person does for a living and try to be helpful. I find out the ideal prospect they look for and how they typically find them. I don't end my time with them by asking, "How can I help you?" I actually come up with an idea I believe would help. At times, the person I'm speaking to will look at me all over again, as if noticing me for the first time, and realize that I had been truly listening, and am trying to be helpful. Listening. That's the key so many sales people miss!

People buy from people they feel they know, like, and trust. If that person happens to be a potential client, I'll make an appointment for another day. Once we've said our goodbyes, I'll write down what I learned from that person. When we meet again, a week or so later, I impress the heck out of the person by remembering much of what he or she shared with me.

At a networking event, the goal is not to meet as many people as possible. Those people meet a lot of folks but never get to know any of them. When attending a networking event, be strategic about what type of person you're seeking out. Look for someone who you feel may be just like you. It's important to know that not everyone in the room is going to provide what you are looking for. Remember, there are a lot more amateurs than professionals out there. Get to know that person and avoid worrying about how many more you need to meet during the event. All it takes is one solid relationship to get your business off and running. It's the age-old rule of quality over quantity.

Depending on what type of sales you're in, the person's job title might dictate who you look for at a networking event. If you're in health or life insurance, perhaps find someone in the property and casualty insurance field. If you're a mortgage broker, a realtor or a financial advisor would be a great strategic partner to have. If you're in automobile sales, build relationships with the people in the service department, people that hear others complain about their cars on a daily basis. Get in there early, and hang around and hear the complaints for yourself. How great would it be to find people currently frustrated with their cars? They have a problem, and you can provide the solution. Too easy!

As a reference, good strategic partners are either business owners or commissioned sales professionals that are in fields where they can't sell your product or service, but where both you and your partner can benefit by cross selling your products or services to your prospects.

To sum up this chapter, prospecting is in and of itself a wide spectrum. Whether you prospect in person, on the phone, via text, or over the Internet, it is absolutely critical to show interest in the other person and not in your sale or yourself. If you work hard, stay focused, prepare, and have true conviction in what you can offer to others, there's no need to fear any part of prospecting from cold calling to setting appointments.

People need your service. Believe it. If you don't believe it, sell something else. Prospecting is simply sifting through the multitude of people and finding those that can use your product or service. That's not a scary thing. You're not a bad person for cold calling; you're a professional salesperson looking to find out who you can help. In helping others, you help yourself.

Notes

Chapter 6

TODAY'S BUYERS

The mindset of a successful salesperson today is one of absolute conviction in the product or service they are selling and an unwavering commitment to helping others. There have been all sorts of sales methodologies that have come and gone, and some that have come and stayed. There's Solution Selling, Spin Selling, the Soft Sell, the Hard Sell, Consultative Selling, the qualifying technique, 100 different closing techniques and more, much more. While many of those techniques can be, and still are, effective, you must understand that today's buyer is more sophisticated and prepared than ever. The more people you help, the more income you earn. It's simple math. To truly build wealth in sales, you must have an unwavering commitment and a strong devotion to helping others.

The more people you help,
the more income you earn
Marco-ism

Today's buyers take their time to review, research, and poll every product out there. This is true for B2C (business to consumer) buyers, as well as B2B (business to business) buyers.

"Not only are B2B buyers taking longer, research-
ing more, and having more people involved in
the purchase process, but they are also giving very
little mindshare to the vendors through the entire
purchase cycle."
Carlos Hidalgo, Annuitas.com

Many salespeople whose products or services aren't the lowest price on the market think that because today's consumer is savvier than ever, they will consistently shop for the lowest price. So, they lose confidence. But that couldn't be further from the truth. Americans will spend money if they feel the value and benefits of a product or service matches or exceeds the price. If it provides a solution for their pain point, then price is less of a factor.

"Buyers today have gone beyond the budget-based
buying of times past; they are sophisticated and
understand the lowest price is not necessarily the
best fit or the best value for their company."
Jack Quarles, author of *Expensive Sentences*.

Sophisticated consumers demand value. They want to buy. They love to buy; they just hate being sold. So… they research. A SearchEngineLand.com post states that 88% of consumers trust online reviews as much as personal reviews. Yelp.com ranks as the 4th largest review site. Check out their numbers:

- 145 Million average monthly unique Yelp visitors
- 2.8 Million claimed local business on Yelp
- 138,000 advertisers on Yelp

Those are impressive numbers wouldn't you say? And there are three other review sites that get more traffic than that!

Whether you are selling B2B or B2C and using any of the aforementioned sales techniques, remember what matters most is not to look, talk, smell, act, or make the prospect think that you're trying to make a sale *for your benefit.*

> *"But Marcos, I am trying to make a sale,*
> *what do I do?"*

That's the problem. You're trying to make a sale, so you're coming across like a salesperson. Remember, people want to buy. They don't want to be sold, and most think the job of a salesperson is to sell... so we sometimes find ourselves in a pickle so to speak.

2 Questions

Prior to making a call, or doing a face to face appointment, I'm not thinking, "how I can sell this person?" My initial thought is, "am I able to help this person?" When I ask myself that question, I am qualifying the prospect first, to see if they would be eligible for my product (budget, credit, health, timeframe, etc.). The second question I ask myself is, "ok, now that I have the answer(s) to that question, in what way can I help him or her?" We all want to make a sale, but only if it's the right option for the prospect and it helps put them in a better position moving forward. I can easily sell 100 people, but it doesn't necessarily mean I helped them. But if I help 100 people, whether it's with my product or I lead them in the direction of someone who can help, then I'm guaranteed to have a 0% chance of hurting someone. Does that make sense? If you genuinely want to help another human being, everything will come naturally, and they will tell you what they need.

A large part of my success is in not making my prospects feel pressured. I make sure they understand that I'm truly looking out for their well-being. I'm knowledgeable in the industry I represent, our services, and the competition; though the only competition you have is yourself. If you're not bringing your "A" game, then you're going to lose out to a selfish amateur who will sell them, regardless of whether or not they are helping that person.

There are times when I am unable to help someone based on qualifying criteria or the simple fact that they are better off with something else. That's not to say I can't sell them. I can sell them, and receive commission dollars for the sale, but it wouldn't necessarily help them. Once I realize that I shouldn't sell my service to someone, I automatically refer him or her to another individual or organization that can, and I move on. Again, it goes back to those initial questions I mentioned earlier.

1. Am I able to help this person?

2. In what way can I help him or her?

By having that mindset, it alleviates any pressure I would otherwise put on myself to close; pressure that would cloud my judgment and surely come across to an intelligent consumer as me being a pushy, selfish, thoughtless salesman. Remember this, you will never feel defeated if you can help another human being, but you can feel defeated if you can't sell to another human being.

The Art of Actually Speaking to the Person You're Calling

The first 10-15 seconds of a sales call is absolutely critical. It's where the person who picks up your call starts the judgment process and asks themselves these questions. Who is this? Do I know this person? Is this a sales call? I've trained countless people who disguised themselves as salespeople during the interview. Initially, I would listen to their phone conversations and cringe during every opening. I won't go into the details of the bad calls I've heard so that I don't put those conversations in your head.

Most salespeople miss the mark in how they start a sales call over the phone. They figure the prospect knows the caller isn't a friend so they feel they need to enter the conversation with a smile because we're taught that people on the phone can hear our smiles and our cheery attitude. Too cheery can come across as too excited. So, they smile and dial away, and promptly get hung up on, or get the "can you call me back?" That's where *call reluctance* starts to creep into the minds of amateurs in every sales organization. If they can overcome the objections, which is achieved by perfect practice, over and over again, they will no longer have call reluctance. They will have call confidence and make more calls. So much in fact, that they'll look forward to objections so they can hone their skillset.

As an aside to this segment, a hang up is kinder than someone telling you to call back when they are just trying to get you off the phone. An amateur salesperson will call back again… and again… and again. And when the salesperson talks to his manager, he'll say, "he asked me to call him back, I'm just trying to get back in touch with him." Really? You got blown off because you came across as a telemarketer. Your manager knows it, the prospect knows it; too bad you don't. In fact, the prospect probably saved your number, using an unflattering name to distinguish you (because they don't know or remember your real name), and will avoid answering your call, hoping you'll get the hint and stop calling. Worse yet, you don't even know if the prospect would qualify or benefit from your product. You have to show posture on the phone and get that information first before you set an appointment to reach them later. Otherwise, you could be spending time and energy trying to reach someone who may not even be a future customer.

In order to be successful on the phone, you have to be someone the person being called *thinks* they know. Note the difference in both of these openings:

"Hello, is this Brendan Smith?"
VS
"Hey, Brendan?"

If you start with, "Hello, is this Brendan Smith?" Mr. Brendan Smith will identify you as a telemarketer, and in a split second, he'll be off the phone.

If you start with, "Hey Brendan?" Brendan's brain will be going a thousand miles a second, trying to pinpoint your voice, wondering how he knows you. He won't be thinking you're a telemarketer. He's unsure, so he will stay on longer while you probe him with more questions.

Brendan might reply with, "Yah, it's Brendan!" or his normal greeting to a friend. You've gotten past stage one to the point in your script where you can introduce who you are then follow up with your first question.

He may ask who it is, or what's this regarding. Be forthcoming, but in a helpful manner. "Looks like one of our folks reached out to you (or looks like you made a request online), what has you looking for this product/service?"

You're now 10 seconds into the call. You didn't get hung up on. You've gotten past the part where call reluctance is usually created, so just keep going. This is where posture starts to set in so have your questions ready and be sure to address all the elephants in the room instead of going to the next question just because it's on your phone script.

If your targeted buyer is in the B2B sector, you might have to get through an administrative assistant – a screener. Here's how not do it. "Hello, is Mr. Henry Johnson available?" Ugh, that's terrible. Sure, it's polite, cordial, respectful, and considerate but it won't get you on the phone with the buyer. Being polite doesn't help people, being a professional does. Ask for them the way you would ask for your friend.

Try this, "Oh hey, is Jacob around?"

The screener doesn't know if you know Jacob personally or if you're trying to get him information on anything. At times, I get patched right through. Win!

At times the screener may ask, "may I tell him who's asking for him?"

I respond, "Yah, it's Marcos calling him back."

In turn, they may also respond by asking, "What is this call pertaining to?"

To this, I answer, "Oh, he'll know what it's about." Now the screener really thinks there's a connection between the two of you. At the risk of possibly losing a future client for that business, the screener will reluctantly transfer the call. Another win for both!

You're never going to help a client with your service if you never talk to them. The purpose of making sales calls is to have sales conversations; it's impossible to have sales conversations if you never get to talk to the people who need what you can offer. This simple method is very effective in getting on the phone with your targeted prospect. It is your obligation to that prospect to use all methods, ethical methods, of course, to get them on the phone, or to meet with you face to face. Your prospects can only benefit from the products or services you can provide if you are able to do your job as a professional.

It is your obligation to each prospect to use every ethical method to speak to them on the phone or in person

Marco-ism

Notes

Chapter 7

PRICE

It's too expensive

"It was too expensive for her."

Not exactly. I hear that all too often from amateurs. Price is almost always never the issue. People have money; they just need to see the value. The focus tends to center on why they didn't buy. The focus should be on how you can help the next prospect see the value you are proposing.

Price is almost never the issue
Marco-ism

Rookie salespeople throw in the towel too quickly when a client say's the product/service costs too much. That's a great objection and one I prefer to hear. They are telling you that the price is too high for the value they are getting in return. Find them more value and price won't be the issue anymore. When value exceeds price, they always buy!

They feel that, since they delivered the features and benefits of a product and then gave the price, the prospect's answer to the "close" signifies whether the call will continue or not. If the prospect declines the offer by stating that it's too expensive, the amateur who has little conviction in what they are offering gets off the phone quickly and dials another number.

The call is not over once the prospect says something is too expensive. He or she has considered the offer... you still have a fighting chance. If I can sit across or talk to 100 people that would seriously consider my products, I'm going to close and help a high number of them. I either close them on why it would benefit them, or they close me on why not. Either way, a sale is being made that day.

Some will side with the client that the product is expensive. Not a good idea unless you believe it is. If that's the case, then your conviction and belief in what you are offering isn't high enough.

Others will say, "We can probably knock the price down." Now the prospect is wondering if you were just trying to sell at a higher price so you could profit in the sale. That response is typically the result of not properly finding out their budget.

I will also hear, "Okay Mr. Smith, I have a cheaper option available that should fit in your price range." Again, the focus is being put on price when it should be on the value. Out of sight out of mind. Your prospect will focus on what you present.

Agreeing that something is too expensive is admitting that you don't believe in the return value your product provides for the price. If you believe that the value your product delivers is more than worth the price for it, you need to do a better job of building the product's value during the presentation. Your product is not expensive; it's worth every penny. You just need to communicate that to the buyer.

I nearly always stick to my proposed price because I wasn't trying to sell the person, I was trying to help them. Here's how I do it:

Don't be Confrontational, Be Agreeable

I never become confrontational by saying, "But you said..." or "Not necessarily"...

I am always agreeable. "I get it. I can see why you want to spend a little less..."

I'm not agreeing that the price is too high; I'm simply agreeing with the prospect, and I understand why they would rather pay less. In their mind, I don't look like someone just trying to make a sale. Once you become disagreeable, their defensive wall comes up, and you will have a harder time reaching through to your prospect and getting them to listen to what you have to say. For the sake of your career, be agreeable!!!!

Everyone wants to pay less. Some of the richest people in the world are some of the most frugal people. I prefer not to pay $150 a month for electricity and would rather pay less, but if I don't, I'll just be uncomfortable in my own house with the A/C set at 83 degrees." We establish the need to pay more than what we would like due to the benefit that we receive.

Sometimes I'll say, "Yah, it isn't for everyone." This releases the pressure of the sale to the prospect. It shows empathy. After all, you're trying to help, not sell. Then I'll say who it's tailor made for, "It's a "no brainer" though for the people that want x, y, and z, and I point out the top benefits. At that point, the prospect is reconsidering it all over again. You're still in the game. As long as you're still in the game, you have an opportunity to come out with a win. When you do win, you go home with the satisfaction of knowing you put someone in a better position after having spoken with you.

Reiterate the value instead of trying to justify the price

"Now, based on what your needs are, this product will provide you the benefits you are looking for."

The next part of the conversation is where most salespeople stumble. They still have the fear of price objection in their mind. Just go in and let them know the investment for the benefit they are seeking. It's not a big deal unless you make it one. If they give you pushback after you mention the price, just quickly acknowledge their concern.

You must have tact to pull this off. "I agree, $300 can be a lot for some folks. However, the only way to have a plan that gives you what you need, based on what you told me, will require this investment. Otherwise, 6 months down the road, you will be regretting your decision to sacrifice value for price. This happened to one client I was trying to help..." and I'll get into a true story of someone not being able to exercise a benefit associated with the plan being offered.

Price is not a big deal unless you make it one
Marco-ism

Then you have to restate the benefits of the product! You are in a pricing disagreement because you fell short of establishing the value. At this point, circle back around and re-establish the value and get them to agree with the statements you're making. Then ask for the sale!

People will agree with value all day long so long as the asking price justifies the return. Remember, price is never the issue.

Offer an Alternative Option

In addition to the option you have already shown them, instead of offering a lower priced solution, offer them a higher priced one. You would be surprised how many will go with the one that costs them more which in return usually offers more value. I use a line I learned from Frank Bettger's book titled "How I raised myself from failure to success in selling" and that is, "if you were my own brother I would encourage you to go with this product because I know it would help you." This statement gets the prospects thinking that maybe they should consider the higher priced product.

By the way, I use this line often –

> *If you were my own father...*
> *If you were my own mother...*
> *If you were my own brother...*
> *If you were my own grandmother...*

I use it because I believe in the value of what I am selling and how it will help that person, so it comes across as genuine, not as an upsell gimmick.

Amateurs are quick to go down in price once they hear the prospect say something is too expensive. "Well, we have a cheaper option for you..." Not the best choice of words. Ever. You want to avoid using the word "cheaper" and going to a lower-priced option. "Hey, I have a cheap watch. Want to buy it?" If the answer is yes, that is not your client. You will never build wealth selling on price alone. Your goal is to find clients that have money. You can't help broke people, and they certainly can't help you.

Always go to a higher-priced option first. If you go to a lower priced option, you lose credibility. The client will wonder why you didn't offer the lower priced one before. By dropping to a lower priced product too quickly, you aren't convincing the prospect that you offered the best value based on what they told you. Now you are solely selling on price, not value. Good luck with that.

Salespeople will also go down in price by reducing some benefits. If the prospect explained to you what they needed and why, why would you sell them something less than what they need? They will think what they are now NOT getting and get dangerously close to finishing the conversation.

If you go to a lower priced option, you simply want to mention that you have another product that might be more affordable yet it comes with fewer benefits.

The prospect will be wondering what coverages are being left out. If they ask, reiterate why you mentioned the first product to begin with. If you've laid a good foundation as someone trying to help instead of someone trying to sell, you'll be discussing the original offer again.

"It's too expensive" is far better than, "I'm not interested."
Marco-ism

When Value Exceeds Price, People Buy

Things are only expensive to a person if he or she doesn't believe the value justifies the price. I can't justify spending $100K on a watch, so I'll think it's expensive. However, people that know about watches and love well-made watches may think that the same watch I thought was too expensive for $100K is well worth it at $100K. Some people pay more for a German car because it is typically made by those who are obsessed with delivering a quality driving machine and the value of that is worth more than the buying price. I have a long time friend of mine who washes exotic sports cars. People from the Tampa Bay area drive to his business and wait for him to wash their cars. I told him he should raise his rates and go mobile; go to people's homes and let them spend the time however they want while he's outside their house or business washing their car. Once he started doing that his business more than tripled.

There's significant value in offering the convenience of time, and people will pay more for it. That's why I pay someone to cut my lawn. I am more than capable of getting a riding lawn mower and mowing my lawn once every two weeks. My time though is better spent on my business and improving my skill set as a salesperson. I'm not necessarily paying for the lawn to be trimmed and cut nicely; I'm paying for MY TIME. I'm paying for me not to spend hours of my day doing manual labor. The price associated with paying my landscapers does not exceed the value they provide by allowing myself to free up valuable time.

That's the same reason I pay for my clothes to get dry-cleaned, my house to be cleaned, or for the service I'll get at Eddie V's or Ruth's Chris while enjoying a fantastic meal. I want to enjoy those things but not spend time on them. We all will pay for what we value. Different people value different things. It manifests itself in different forms; it could be time, expertise, experience, peace of mind, etc. I recently paid nearly double for a haircut because the salon was in the same building as where I had a meeting, and I didn't have the time to drive halfway across the city to get a haircut from my normal barber. The price was double what I normally pay, but I paid it because it offered me convenience and time and that exceeded the price.

When people tell you the price you quoted was too expensive... think about it. Do you really think that's the case?

If they have no money, the price still wasn't too expensive. They just don't have the money! You have to find out if they're financially able to purchase your products before you give the price though. Don't spend a lot of time with people who have no money. Again, you can't help them.

Notes

Chapter 8

FAIR ENOUGH?

Fair Enough?

During a sales call there will be moments where you will want your prospect to feel that you are either sacrificing time or willing to work with them in some manner in order to be open to what you are presenting or asking. Some people do it so blatantly that instead of it building trust, the prospect builds a wall. "Would you agree that...?" That's something that a lawyer might ask you if you're on trial. No one wants to be cross-examined, knowing that everything they say will be turned against them. I use, "fair enough?"

"Before we submit this application, is there any reason why you wouldn't follow through if you were approved? All I ask is that you address any concerns you may have. Fair enough?"

In all my years of sales, no one has ever said, "No, that's not fair."

When they tell me it's 'fair enough,' either with an okay or a grunt, they just acknowledged our first agreement. It's a buying signal that the client has a clear interest and understands I am giving instead of taking away. Every time

I say something and can end it with, 'fair enough?' the topic I had just mentioned becomes less of an issue. They have agreed that I have properly explained the topic in a manner that currently satisfies their curiosity and I have been granted permission to move on.

The obvious goal is to encourage them to say yes. You're not manipulating them. You are getting answers to your questions that will help you, help them.

When Discussing the Competition

"This sounds good Marcos, but before I make decisions I want to check out all my options, so I'm going to check out the competition and then get back to you."

#1 rule of sales competition etiquette: don't bash the competition. Ever. What are you afraid of? If you start making a stink about the competition, then they will see you have something to fear and that you will do whatever it takes to benefit you in a sale.

Don't bash your competition. Ever.
Marco-ism

I'm not saying to get off the phone that easily either. You acknowledge their intentions and respond in kind: "I can see why you would want to do that and if you have the time to do it, I understand." Time is something I can save you though. Is there something else that you are looking for?"

Most people would rather not go through the same type of conversation with someone else only to end up spending more of their precious time.

"I'm just here to help you take advantage of a product that will definitely provide you with what you're looking for. Was I able to do that for you?"

If you didn't, the prospect will tell you why they still want to look somewhere else. Chances are, you did. At that point, you've earned the right to go for the close.

At times, I bring up the competition. (It should go without saying that if you're going to bring up the competition yourself that you know their products and pricing about as well as you know yours.) "Have you had the chance to check out XYZ Company?" If they say yes, "What did you find out?" There is a lot that the prospect will teach you on how to go about helping him or her. You might hear:

The sales guy was too pushy
I liked the convenience of their service
I told them I was going to meet with you and get back to them
I wasn't ready to buy at the time

Once you understand what they liked and didn't, it should be easier for you to move through the sales process. It's almost as if they are giving you a roadmap with clear highways and pot holes to watch out for. If they say, "It was too expensive." I ask, "When you say too expensive, is it that you couldn't afford it or it was not worth the price they were asking?" Again, it's about the value, not the price. So, you know when you present that person a product or service to emphasize the value. "I've heard that before about them. I'll make sure to present you with something you're going to feel is worth the asking price, fair enough?"

Many prospects are more up to date with industry information than the actual sales people in the industry. Rookies refute this as if they feel that because they're the experts, only what they say is true. So they disagree with what they're being told. I agree with everything. I act surprised, as if they taught me something.

The reason is that they already believe it. Why fight it? Why put yourself on the other side of the fence on a topic.

I act as if it caught me off guard. "Wow. Really? I wasn't aware of that." It empowers the prospect because now you are having a back and forth conversation and it's not so much of an interrogation.

If it's something negative about my company or about a similar product I sell, I say, "Hmmm, I've never heard of anything like that happening before. I can't really explain why something like that would happen. All I can tell you, because this is about me and you, what I'm offering you has helped every single one of my clients in the past. All I ask is that we keep the communication line open and if you ever run into a problem anywhere close to that in the future, I'll address it. Fair enough?"

It's all about setting the right expectations.

People like to know that after the sale you are still going to be there. Sure, you probably have an excellent customer service team. However, the prospect is buying from you, not them. They don't want the Wham Bam sale, and then you forget their name. Always be available. Always.

When a client brings up something negative, don't get defensive and don't make excuses. Narrow the focus down to the relationship between the two of you, give testimonials, and then follow with a personal commitment to always be there to help. That's all people want. Someone to reach out to in a time of need.

Amateurs feel that the world is full of competitors. It's not. Not if you're just trying to help people.

Be an Ask-Hole

The beauty of two and three-year-old children is in their inquisitiveness and persistence. They have an insatiable need to know the world around them. Why seems to be their favorite "go to" word.

"Why is the sky blue?"

"Why does the apple fall from the tree?"

"Why can't I have more candy?"

"Why don't cars fly?"

It's not that they don't believe what the parent is teaching them, they just want to know why it's true. They want to know the reason behind how things operate. To be successful in sales, you also need to know the reasons behind the prospects answers. Like a child, be inquisitive. Ask 'why,' 'when,' and 'what' questions until you have all the answers you need before moving on to the next phase of the sales process.

"Mr. Cruz, what has you looking for insurance today."

"I'm shopping around."

"Why are you shopping around?"

"I actually don't have insurance, and I'm deciding which company to choose."

"Ah, you're doing your homework. I respect that. Why don't you have insurance right now though?"

"Last time I was looking for some, it was too expensive?"

"When was that?"

"About three years ago."

"What's changed with you that after three years you are looking again?"

"I'm married now and want to make sure my wife has coverage."

In that short conversation, I learned that Mr. Cruz is shopping around. That's his way of telling me he does not want to be pressured into making a decision. I also learned he doesn't have insurance because he feels it's too expensive, which tells me Mr. Cruz might not have the money to buy insurance. Also, his wife might have some medical issues or upcoming medical issues for which he wants coverage.

Asking why, when, and what questions are like asking for coordinates to a location. Once you know how to get to a location, all you need to do is execute your skills, and you should be able to help your prospects.

Notes

Chapter 9

WHAT TYPE OF CLOSER ARE YOU?

So, let's talk about what type of closers are in the marketplace. Salespeople usually fall into three different types of categories: soft closers, hard closers, and assumptive closers.

Soft Closers

Another term for them is order takers. They're anxious when doing their job. These are the type of salespeople that, after making seven calls: including getting hung up on twice, and one caller telling them "I'm all set," lose confidence and develop what's known in the industry as call reluctance. They go get another cup of coffee, tell the person next to them how bad the leads are, or check their emails (usually personal emails, these people don't receive too many business emails). They typically are not good at setting up the context for the sales conversation and have difficulty staying on the path to a sale. When it comes time for them to *close,* they are unprepared and nervous. Worse yet, they repeat amateurish mistakes over and over.

They allow themselves to think that they need to be nice, so they are not going to be pushy. But if they believed in their product and that what they are selling is exactly what the prospect needs, they wouldn't be reluctant to ask for the close because they wouldn't view themselves as pushy, they would view themselves as helpful.

They end up being sheep, and sheep get led. Soft closers have no posture and allow the prospect to have all the control. Every time the prospect raises an objection, the soft closer tends to get defensive. They aren't sure what to reply with and hastily search for an answer but fail to come up with an appropriate response. If you are unable to predict what the prospect will respond with, you will never get to the level you wish to achieve.

Soft closers are sheep, and sheep get led.
Marco-ism

Nothing frustrates sales managers more than a soft closer. They invest valuable resources that would be better spent on the ones who know how to close. The worst part is, their clients usually suffer from buyers-remorse and cancel their deals within 48 hours of signing the agreement!

People misunderstand the very concept of the soft sale. A soft sale, in basic terms, is where the salesperson offers a product but without being pushy. Almost to the point where it's okay if the prospect wants to think about it or shop around for other options. Well, it's not okay. Your prospects don't benefit from information; they only benefit if they have or use your product so long as it's a solution to their problem.

A few months ago, while spending a weekend with my father, I decided to visit a Mercedes-Benz dealership near him. I was interested to know more about the recently released Mercedes AMG GT-S. I immediately asked to speak with an AMG representative. These are usually the highly trained sales professionals who have earned the right to sell the AMG brand. The salesman greeted me, and I told him the car I wanted to look at.

"Is that your Porsche 911 outside?" he asked.

"Sure is, I bought it not too long ago,"

"Well, the good news is that the AMG GT-S destroys your Porsche in just about every area," he said, quite smugly.

First rule of thumb: never bash what your client currently has! Ever! You're basically telling them that they made a poor decision. It's condescending, which is never a good way to start the sales process. People do business with people they feel like they know, like, and trust. I was certainly not starting to like him.

He led me to where the AMG GT-S was in the showroom and proceeded to drop information on me. All I really wanted to do was sit in the car though. He didn't get the hint, even after I attempted to open the doors of the car.

"Can you open it so I can sit inside?" I asked.

"Of course."

Then he realized he didn't have the key, so I had to wait for him to stroll away to get it, stopping to chat quickly with a co-worker. As I sat in the car, the salesman just stood there waiting for my response. I really liked the car, but he was doing very little to get me to buy it, so I decided to help the guy out and give him a few closing questions. I first asked how much of a deposit they would need if I wanted to order the car. He answered but did so without a follow-up question. I then asked how long it would take for the car to arrive.

"8-10 weeks,"

But again, no follow up question. I gave him one more opportunity and asked if it would be a 2017 or 2018 model.

He responded that it would be a 2018. At that point, I was thinking, he either doesn't sell many cars or feels his product is in some way above me.

As much as I liked the car, he simply didn't earn my business or the business of those I would have referred to him. If he simply would have asked follow-up questions I probably would have bought another car that day. He made the single most common mistake that any soft closer repeats. He was expecting me to make the sale. Prospects never make the sale, they only buy. The salesperson always makes the sale.

Many soft closers can get through the presentation just fine until it's time to get the signature or payment information. It's at that point that they start getting a little nervous knowing they have to ask for the payment.

Soft Closer: "Ok, so you agree that this is what you're looking for, right?"

Prospect: "I think so, I just need some time to think about it."

Soft Closer: "What is it you want to think about?"

A five-second silence ensues, it's not an uncomfortable silence, it's just that both parties are waiting for the other to speak. The sales person is waiting for even more confirmation that the prospect wants the product.

Soft Closer: "Ok, so if we agree... are there any other questions you might have?"

Prospect: "Hmmm (now he's thinking the sales person is giving him an out. Why would he do that?) Is there anything you haven't told me that I need to know?"

The soft closer starts to get anxious and getting that feeling that they are about to lose the sale. Was the prospect not sold on the product or on me? Oh no!

Go for the close already!!! Tell him the price or the next step to either receiving or applying for what you are offering. *Sorry, I couldn't take my own analogy without exploding. These types of calls are infuriating to me though.*

Hard Closers

Hard closers typically possess more confidence in what they are selling or have been in their field for years. The hard close is a very popular type of close, but not everyone can pull it off. It takes a certain balance of directness mixed in with some tact and playfulness. Of course, you never have the right to be a hard closing jerk, but the prospect also shouldn't have the right to waste your time; especially when they can truly benefit from what you are offering.

You never have the right to be a hard closing jerk.
Marco-ism

I remember being out at dinner one time. I arrived a few minutes earlier than my friends, and there was a pretty long wait up front at the hostess stand, so I sidled up to the bar. The bartender was pretty busy but got to me when he could. I asked him for the different types of vodka they served.

"Are you in the mood for cheap, strong, what's popular or something different, like a mojito?"

"You know, I usually go with the house vodka but tell me what other types you have?"

He gave me a few options, but after several minutes, I still hadn't decided. I was looking at one of the nicer bottles at the bar which was probably higher priced than the others, when he interrupted me, "Hey man, I have to grab some drinks for that other group that just came in. Just order that one (he pointed at a bottle of Kettle One), you're gonna like it."

I felt like I was too undecided and had taken his time so I quickly agreed with him. It wasn't until some days later that I realized he Hard Closed me. But guess what, I didn't take umbrage to it, not at all. You know what? The people you use the hard close tactic on if you do it right, won't be offended either.

The Hard Close has a bad rap. People hear it and think hard closers are pushy salespeople that are only looking out for their own interests. Those aren't Hard Closers; those are selfish salespeople. Hard Closers are people that directly ask for the order. Using the same scenario as I did with the Soft Closer, this is how Hard Closers typically close:

Hard Closer: "OK Mr. Cannon. It looks like we found you what you're looking for. I need you to authorize the order here."

Prospect: "Well, I haven't decided."

Hard Closer: "Why wait? Let's get the contract signed and start enjoying the *"benefits of the product."*

Prospect: "Can I cancel if I change my mind?"

Hard Closer: "No one cancels with me. Not once they see how good this product is. I got a busy day today; I know you can appreciate that. We've talked about this at length, and I think I answered all your questions to your satisfaction, right?"

Prospect nods
Hard Closer: "Great. Just sign here…"

It's okay to let your prospect know that you fully believe in your product and you're a busy person. When the bartender told me he was busy and either I ordered now or he was going to take orders from people that were ready to order, well, I bought the drink he recommended.

We live in a time of the conscientious consumer. Not only are we more educated than ever before in the history of humankind due to the rampant information online – Yelp, blogs, social media, news outlets; but we're also more aware. We know things that the previous generation didn't think of, such as human growth hormones, blood diamonds, slave labor, and different forms of pesticides. We as people are more aware of the world around us like never before. In the same vein, we know when we are taking up a salespersons time. They know you're working on commission. It's not a secret. They also know if they intend to buy or not much sooner than they let on. So, it's fair to let the prospect know your time is valuable and, if you've answered their questions to their satisfaction, you'd like to close on the sale.

What gives Hard Closers a bad reputation are those that try to close everybody, people that need the product and those that really don't. They over-talk and, at times, make the prospect reluctant to have an objection, feel dumb if they have to ask a question or admit they don't have enough money. Really hard closers typically have a high cancellation rate. They push prospects to buy, and once the sale is over, the prospects figure out they've been sold something they don't need and then cancel. Numbers on the board mean nothing unless it's paid business.

"Numbers on the board mean nothing unless it's
paid business"
Marco-ism

My official stance on hard closers is that they do a good job of getting sales. They're not afraid to get on the phones or make appointments. They're also not afraid to go for the close and ask for the order. However, I'm not a fan of those that are selfish, the ones that try to sell and not help. There's a fine line to that and one which I'm not willing to cross. I think there's a better method. That method is the role of the Assumptive Closer.

Assumptive Closers

While I don't like to label myself as a particular style of closer, I align more with this type of close than the other two. Many say assumptive closers "act as if" the prospect is going to buy. I don't act as if someone is going to buy; I believe they are going to buy. If I answered their questions, cleared their objections, and agreed with the prospect that the value of my product exceeds the price, why would I not believe they are going to buy?

Before I get to the end of the sales cycle, I make sure I've addressed every elephant in the room. If at the end of my presentation a prospect asks me if he can cancel, I realize that I must have missed an elephant or two. It might be just one thing, and the prospect is still planning on buying. I just need to find out what it is.

"Sure you can cancel the order, but let's address the reason why you just asked that question. It's usually a simple reason, and I want to make sure you have the right expectation regarding how this product will work for you. Fair enough?

I will then recap the features and benefits and ask confirmation questions along the way to ensure the prospect is still following along and is interested. I'll usually end with a popular line used by Frank Bettger, author of "How I Raised Myself From Failure To Success In Selling." "If you were my own brother, (father, mother, sister, grandmother) in your same situation, I would tell him what I'm going to tell you now."

You know what I don't hear? More questions regarding canceling. Because they realize I'm not trying to sell them, I'm trying to help them. You know what I don't get? Cancellations. People I help understand that they got something of great value at a cost comfortable for them.

Notes

Chapter 10

TRUST ISSUES

It's all about the close

It's all about the close. That's the objective. Everything you do on a sales call, whether it be one conversation over the phone, multiple presentations, or yearlong meetings with CFO's and CEO's, it should always lead to an agreement resulting in a sale. Without the close, there's no sale. Without the sale, there's no payment for services. Without a payment for services, there's no commission check. Yes, a commission check. If you are in sales, you shouldn't be working for a salary. Ever. If you are on a salary, you have already limited your potential growth and effectively put a cap on your income earnings. The fact is, the most highly paid sales people I know have never had a salary. Getting paid based on their results to deliver is all they ever knew. That's all I ever knew and will ever know. Nobody will be able to pay me what I'm truly worth. You should feel strongly about that as well. If you can't deliver, you either need to learn quickly how to close and find conviction in what you are selling or find another career besides sales. If not, you only end up wasting your time and taking away valuable resources from the professionals.

Repeat Sales

If you sell in a vertical that can grant you repeat customers, consider yourself perfectly positioned. You have a dream sales job! I'll tell you why; you are in a position where you can get additional revenues without having to cold call, qualify, or close. All you have to do is treat the client with respect, dignity, and professionalism.

Make sure to keep tabs on your clients after the sale. Make sure they're happy with whatever it was they bought from you. Set a reminder on your phone or appointment book to text, call, or email them. Those people are more important to you than your prospects. They are the key holders to referrals, and referrals are the lifeblood of many sales jobs. It's much easier to get referrals than it is to get new business. But remember, they will only send you referrals if you keep reminding them you're there and, this is very important, you need to ask for it. People will help out people that have helped them.

"It's much easier to get referrals than it is to get new business"
Marco-ism

"I need to think about it"

For those of you who don't know Grant Cardone , I highly recommend that you read his books. He is an extraordinary sales trainer, speaker, author, and more. I love Grant. I don' t just read his books ; armed with a highlighter , I scour through them for nuggets of information I can assimilate into my work life. I also watch his videos, as many as I can. He has an effective comeback to the age-old prospect delay tactic of – I need to think about it.

First, he identifies it as an objection. See, many others don't see it that way. They feel that they have had great dialogue with the prospect and have given him or her a price they said they could afford. So, when they hear, "I need to think about it," they don't realize that the person is nearly ready to be helped, he or she just needs a bit more assurance. Or they are simply just adding time to their decision making.

Grant answers that question with, "Sure, do you need 2 or 3 days or 2 or 3 weeks?" He's being agreeable, not pushy. Sales people in the 80's were taught to be much more direct. "What do you need to think about?" and have lost potential sale after potential sale.

"3 days? Excellent." He's being agreeable again, not pushy. "Days or weeks, I've found that it comes down to 3 questions. Mind if I share them with you real quick?" Now he's being helpful. He's not repeating any features, benefits or the great price; he's just trying to help. At this point, no one is going to say, "No, don't share them with me!"

Once he gets agreement to share the 3 questions, he says:

1. Do you feel this product will provide you with what your family needs?

2. Do you believe you could easily afford this product based on your budget? (Which is a great question because many stalls happen during the pricing portion of a presentation and now you have time to address it with the client, which is better for both of you than if the prospect just focused on the money without you.)

3. Do you feel that I am the type of person you'd like to help you out with your future needs? (They always say yes to this one, always.)

If the answers are all yes, they were just looking for reassurance. It's human nature. We're told not to be sold, not to make a quick decision, especially during a first call. But if that all sounds good to them and you work for a reputable company, feel free to go for the close again.

"Ok great! You just saved yourself three days of thinking about it and can now focus on things that are more important. Here's what's going to happen next. We will fill out this order so that now you'll save time, and can experience the benefit of the products sooner."

"I Don't Trust Salespeople"

Your prospects may never say that to you, but they feel that way. Unfortunately, for us, not all sales people have integrity and look to help others. My experience in sales is that there are too many amateurs out there trying to make a quick buck and flash sales numbers. That is what we are up against. Sales at any cost, which usually comes at the cost of the customer. If you realize that the person on the other end of the phone, desk, Starbucks table, or computer screen doesn't trust you, and you never address it, it's going to be an uphill climb to get the close and help that person.

That is why it's imperative to ensure that you come across as sincere and empathetic when needed. It's important to listen to those subtle clues as to why the prospect is looking for your product. Find out what has them looking and ask what about the previous product they liked or didn't like.

Distrust only becomes an issue if you allow it. Make sure they know who you are and why you do what you do. Show them your credentials, when possible, before you get into your presentation. If applicable, let them know that you own the same product you are offering them. They will see that you believe in the product so much that you were willing to purchase it yourself. In the end, you help people, plain and simple. You help them with a solution to their problem, you save them time, and you help them afford what they need. If you can do that, sales is - Too Easy.

You can't help broke people

The prospect obviously didn't see the value of what was covered, or they simply don't have money. Sales people who have different "pricing buckets" or who can lower their price, usually look bad here. Amateurs will lower the price without hesitation; they just want to make the sale. Here's a hard truth for some sales people, you can't help those that are broke.

"We can't help broke people."
Marco-ism

Some people never feel like they got a good deal if they purchase at full price. They think no one pays full retail price. If you're good at what you do, they all do.

If it's a legitimate concern, you can come down on price so long as you don't offer as many features or benefits. A price reduction should amount to fewer benefits. If you make a habit of dropping your price in order to close, you're not really a closer and you're not going to make real closer money. Nor will you help people the way you should.

It might not be a price issue of the product; it might be a money issue for the prospect. You have to find out what it is.

"If this is going to be difficult for you to pay, I can offer up another option for you. I offered this solution for you based on what you said you needed. The other option won't have all of the benefits we spoke about but I'd rather you get into something that's going to be easy to afford."

If you let people nickel and dime you, you will make nickel and dime paychecks.

Here is where trust in your company comes into play. You have to trust that they have adequately priced your products. You have to trust their track record of people that have purchased at the price you asked for.

"Mr. Smith, this is our top-moving product because, quite candidly, it offers the most benefit for the money. I understand that the price seems high to you, but if you were my own father, this is what I'd be offering you. Do you see how it can help you?" Bam, I'm right back to the close!

Baseball players get three strikes before they strike out. I wonder why some sales people don't take three swings at closing to get their asking price. If you want to **earn** the big bucks, don't give up after one miss; swing away.

Notes

Chapter 11

BEAST MODE

ABC's of Closing

A scene from the movie Glengarry Glen Ross, (a 1992 American drama film adapted by David Mamet from his 1984 Pulitzer Prize, directed by James Foley.)

I'm going to change some words to make it PG-13...

Blake: Let me have your attention for a moment! So you're talking about what? You're talking about... (puts out his cigarette)... bitching about that sale you shot, some guy that doesn't want to buy, somebody that doesn't want what you're selling, some broad you're trying to hook up with and so forth. Let's talk about something important. Are they all here?

Williamson: All but one.

Blake: Well, I'm going anyway. Let's talk about something important! (to Levene) Put that coffee down!! Coffee's for closers only. (Levene scoffs) Do you think I'm messing with you? I am not messing with you. I'm here from downtown. I'm here from Mitch and Murray. And I'm here on a mission of mercy. Your name's Levene?

Levene: Yeah.

Blake: You call yourself a salesman, you son of a b**ch?

Moss: I don't have to listen to this stuff.

Blake: You certainly don't pal. 'Cause the good news is -- you're fired. The bad news is you've got, all you got, just one week to regain your jobs, starting tonight. Starting with tonight's sit. Oh, have I got your attention now? Good. 'Cause we're adding a little something to this months sales contest. As you all know, first prize is a Cadillac Eldorado. Anyone want to see second prize? Second prize's a set of steak knives. Third prize is you're fired. You get the picture? You're laughing now? You got leads. Mitch and Murray paid good money. Get their names to sell them! You can't close the leads you're given, you can't close crap, you ARE crap, hit the bricks pal and beat it 'cause you are going out!!!

Levene: The leads are weak.

Blake: 'The leads are weak.' Freaking leads are weak? You're weak. I've been in this business fifteen years.

Moss: What's your name?

Blake: Screw YOU, that's my name!! You know why, Mister? 'Cause you drove a Hyundai to get here tonight, I drove an $80,000 BMW. That's my name!!

Alex Baldwin's portrayal as the hard-nosed closer, Blake, in Glengarry Glen Ross still resonates with many people today. In my opinion, the most candid speech ever given on sales in any film I've seen. In the year 1992, an $80,000 car was quite expensive. Today that same speech would probably be given referencing a Mercedes S Class or a Porsche Panamera (sorry, I'm a 'car guy'). The point was that he was obviously successful and had to motivate people to want to become successful.

In the movie, he goes on to share the ABC's of sales – Always Be Closing. The ABC's of sales have been taught in both large and small sales organizations all over the world. It's the most powerful 3-letter acronym in sales. That's because it works.

Many people in sales think, "How can I always be closing? First I have to introduce myself, break the ice, engage with the prospect, uncover their pain, get them to tell me their budget, and then provide a solution! I can't go for the close until I do all that." Those are the order takers, not closers. You can't afford to think like that. Your career and livelihood depend on it!

The secret is, great closers are always closing!!! The Close is nothing more than a formality or agreement. Once you have taken a prospect through the conversation I have laid out in this book, all there is to do next is take care of the paperwork.

I don't have a classic closing line. I just go in based on the conversation; I assume that the next natural step is to get the prospect signed up. I say, "So by getting started today, your policy will come into effect as soon as you are approved. I'll need your payment information and your authorization here." They already know the pricing and the benefits. In addition to that, they agreed that it all was "fair enough" so I make it easy for them to go on with their lives and enjoy the benefits of the products I have access to. Too Easy.

Beast Mode

You must go into your sales calls with a relentless call to action. Reaching as many prospects as possible, so you have a higher number to present your product to. Someone once told me I close, "Like a Boss." I suppose that's a popular saying right now. While I guess it's a compliment, I don't think I sell like a boss. I let my leadership instincts kick in and guide my prospects to an ethical, affordable solution. It's that simple. Those who lack in skill (amateurs) can make up for that in activity, huge amounts of activity.

I'd rather be known as a person that rolls up his sleeves, puts the blinders on and focuses on large amounts of activity. Be a beast on the phones. A beast just doesn't care; it runs through obstacles and devours whatever stands in its way. Tom Brady is a beast. He's a 6-time Super Bowl winning quarterback , has won 4 Super Bowl MVP awards - the most ever by a single player, 2 league MVP awards, been selected to 13 Pro Bowls, and has led his team to 15 division titles, more than any other quarterback in NFL history . The Patriots ' owner , Robert Kraft is the boss. The Patriots ' head coach Bill Belichick calls the shots, so he's like the second boss. Brady, as great as he is, isn't the boss... he's a beast. He's relentless in his pursuit of perfection and the success of his career.

Beasts run through obstacles and devour whatever stands in its way.
Marco-ism

Professionals like Tom Brady have a different mentality than most others. Where others see little opportunity (in sales, that might be old leads, people who say it's too expensive, or those who thank them for their time but now they're going to shop around), beasts see vast amounts of opportunity. Beasts are insatiable; they're not satisfied with being at the top of the leaderboard if they haven't broken the sales record. They always want to be better than they were the day before. They are never content with where they are. Beast mode. That's all they know.

Fear of Rejection? It's a myth!

They don't fear rejection in sales because it actually doesn't exist in sales. Many salespeople that never make big money think that they need to get rejected over and over again in order to get a sale. It's one of the most common modes of thinking. And while I agree wholeheartedly that it's a number's game, meaning you have to contact many people before getting a sale, I don't believe I get rejected. When someone doesn't join into a partnership with me or my company, I don't feel that I've lost a sale. I never had the sale to begin with! How can I lose it? So I never let that thought enter my mind.

That mode of thinking is dangerous because, after a while, you feel as you keep getting rejected over and over and over again. You start to believe that you aren't good at what you do or that the products you're representing aren't valuable to the marketplace. If the top saleswoman for a company closes 10 percent of the people she talks to in a given day and earns a substantial income from her sales, should she go home feeling that she gets beaten up 90 percent of the day? Just because sales organizations label a closed deal a win, doesn't mean that every other call was a loss. Does that make sense?

"How can you lose a sale you never had?"
Marco-ism

When you initiate a sales conversation, whether it's in your office, at the car lot, over the phone, or via live video, you don't have the sale. If at the end of the conversation, the prospect doesn't go through with the purchase order, guess what, you still don't have the sale. But you didn't lose it because you never had it.

It's as if a man makes a reservation at a restaurant, and then asks a woman out to dinner, but she declines. Did he lose the table at the restaurant? Can't he still go there and have a nice dinner? Sure he can. He didn't lose the reservation. He's just going to dine alone.

Some sales people in today's organizations are timid and soft. They think like sheep and get angry when the beasts of the office are ringing bells, helping more people, smashing records, and earning large amounts of income based on their efforts. The sheep gather to talk about the top earners behind their backs.

"He's so arrogant."

"She's so conceited; she never stops talking about her success!"

"No wonder he's in first place, he lives for this place!"

"She rarely goes out to lunch with us, what's her problem?"

The truth is, there isn't a problem, there's a difference. Some are sheep, and those making a ton of money are beasts. Those who are winning are just committed to their career and won't let anyone or anything stand in their way of achieving their goals.

Unfortunately, not many salespeople realize that they should be doing what the top earners are doing. So they sit with them, ask for their advice and come away with the type of information that could transform their financial lives… only to do the same things and have the same mindset. They speak into their phones with the same weak lines, "So, how can I help you?"

"Act as if…"

If you think you're working off of bad leads, you have to believe as if you're not.

If the product you sell is too expensive for you to buy, you must believe as if it's not too expensive for your prospects.

If you're in the middle of a sales call and you've already had to overcome three objections, but you're still on the call, you have to believe as if you've overcome all the hurdles and now it's a matter of getting to the agreement of the sale.

If you state your name and company and the other person hangs up on you, you need to handle it as if it was not personal, because it wasn't.

If you've had a bad couple of days or a bad week, you need to go to work the following day believing as if this is the day things turn around for you, the day you get out of your slump.

You absolutely must believe as if you're a beast, not a sheep; as if nothing can stop you from obtaining your goals. As if you were put on this earth to help people by getting them the products you're selling. As if the other person across from you has no idea that he or she is dealing with a highly motivated, knowledgeable, sympathetic, caring professional and that person has no way of not seeing the value your product or service will provide.

Grant Cardone? Beast

Brian Tracey? Beast

Simon Sinek? Beast

Marcos Figueroa? Well, you get the point.

Whether you believe I belong on this list has no bearings on how I believe I belong on this list. Where does your name belong? On this list or the list of sheep?

If you've always been a reserved, quiet, bashful sales amateur, now is an opportune time for you to change up your game. Change your mindset in such a manner that it manifests into different actions, so you become a beast. We have a different perspective on what represents an opportunity and how we will go about making things happen. For us, an opportunity is in every single sales meeting, and every single sales call. Every. Single. One.

Flip the proverbial mental switch and get into Beast Mode. I promise you it'll change your life.

Notes

Chapter 12

UNBORN OPPORTUNITY

It's not for you to try

Earning six figures in sales in not rocket science . It's a mixture of mindset, attitude, the willingness to work for it, some technique, and by not being afraid to ask for the deal . The problem is that most people will read this , implement some of it, experience minimal gains, and then revert back to their old ways. I hope that's not what you are going to do.

Everything I've taught to this point is not for you to *try,* it's for you to incorporate. Your present habits have brought you to a point where you're reading a book on how to make six figures because you're currently not. The only way to make more money at your current position is to turn your present habits into old habits.

It starts with your mindset. Stop thinking you're trying to sell people and believe you're trying to help people. Keep the main reason why you want to make serious money; your *WHY,* in the forefront of your mind. Use a goal board, a vision board, a pop up on your computer, a sticky note on your bathroom mirror, whatever it takes to keep the desire burning in you to be wildly successful. Your why is the gas that keeps your motor percolating.

Build on what you've learned. Remember, you don't get paid for what you know, you get paid for what you do. If your activity level is already high, all you need is to match it with the right skill set. If your skill set is high, all you need to do is match it with the right activity level.

Unborn Opportunity

Every single day that you have the privilege of helping someone through the products and services you sell understand that there is unborn opportunity all around you. I love being in sales for that very reason. On any given day, I can create opportunity out of what others see as nothing; out of old leads, out of disgruntled clients, and even out of a saturated market. I'm too stubborn, too focused to see anything but opportunity.

Napoleon Hill wrote, in his book, Think and Grow Rich: "We who desire to accumulate riches, should remember the real leaders of the world have always been people who harnessed, and put into practical use, the intangible, unseen forces of unborn opportunity."

My question is, what do you see when you walk into the office? Those that think, "Oh well, another day at the office," will never make much more money than they do now.

Napoleon Hill also wrote, "There is one quality which one must possess to win, and that is DEFINITENESS OF PURPOSE, the knowledge of what one wants, and the burning DESIRE to possess it.

Incorporate what I've taught in this book, many of these concepts are not new, they've been tried and are proven to work. I have read countless sales and motivational books in my adult life. I've taken the best of what I've learned and paired it with the things I have done to crush six figures with ease, year, after year, after year. If you take your career seriously, you can as well. Then you can do what I'm doing now – show others how to do it!

Become a mentor in your organization, on the sales floor, in the bullpen, or wherever you help your prospects. By becoming a leader, when people look up to you, you feel more confident. You become more secure about what you're doing for your company. Leadership forces you, just as much as anything, to perform. Your coworkers, your team, your managers, your CEO, will hold you accountable once you start getting pats on the back. They'll expect that you will never be a flash in the pan and that you'll continue to lead the company to new heights.

Success is a great motivator, but it should also come with a Warning Label. When you start to crush it, you start to get more accolades, more opportunities, and more power.

> *"Nearly all men can stand adversity, but if you want to test a man's character, give him power."*
> **Abraham Lincoln**

Make sure when you start climbing the ladder of success that it doesn't change your habits. Success makes you act differently, talk differently, spend your time differently, dress differently, just make sure it doesn't change the things that made you successful. I'm still waking up at the same times as I was when I decided to change my life.

Just because I have money, I've won numerous awards, and I oversee two thriving offices, doesn't mean that I can take my foot off the gas. On the contrary, it makes me hungrier. Beasts are never satiated. I'm just as hungry now for people that report to me to make the type of money I make. I'm hungry to take my locations and establish them on the top of the food chain in my organization. I'm hungry to develop and train sales professionals that surpass my earnings. I'm hungry to add two more zeroes to my annual earnings. What are you hungry for?

If you don't feel the same as the vibe coming from this book, you might need to surround yourself with other people. Associate yourself with the type of people that are chasing their dreams.

The Truth about Legacies

Work hard now so your life is better sooner rather than later. Screw later! Make life better as soon as you can. Why deny yourself a better way of life?

"I'm working to leave a legacy..." Screw that! I'm not trying to leave a legacy for when I'm dead. I'm working to build my legacy while I'm alive. Today I donate money to Veterans Organizations, mission trips, and to aid disaster victims. I get immense pleasure knowing that I'm helping people. I'm actively a part of the legacy I'm leaving behind, and it feels wonderful.

I'm working to leave a legacy while I'm alive
Marco-ism

You get many second chances in life but not with your time. I often want to shake people and yell, "Wake up! Your life is passing you by!" We can't get our time back so use it wisely.

You don't have a reset button in life. Be selfish about making enough money so that you can help others. If you can live comfortably on $60K, why not strive to earn $120K and help others with the extra money? Givers gain, the more you give, the more you get back.

The Truth about Money

Money runs its own patterns. You need to operate under the belief that there is an abundance of money because there is. There's plenty for everybody. People that base their decisions on a mindset that there is a scarcity of money handicap their earning potential.

There's plenty of money for everybody
Marco-ism

Open your thinking up to the realization that money is flowing freely around the world. Billions of dollars are exchanged every ten minutes. I never worry about how much I give away because I will make plenty more. Money loves me. I'm a conduit for it. It comes to me in bunches, and I invest it in myself to make more, I invest it in my offices for others to make more than ever before, I invest it in people in need. Money and I have an understanding; I'll respect it, and work hard for it, and it will continue to find its way to me.

I'd rather not have tens or hundreds of thousands of dollars saved in my treasure chest (bank) collecting 1% interest. People that hoard their money seem to be waiting for when things inevitably go bad. I believe that if I invest it in me getting better, I'll never need a rainy day fund.

The single best investment one can make is in one's self. Invest time into acquiring sales habits that will change your life. Put the time in to reach your goals. When I was "on the rise" I worked weekends, I didn't take Saturday's and Sundays off. I worked when others didn't, or better said when others wouldn't. Now that I've been crushing the six-figure mark year after year, I still work weekends. I will not be outworked. Sales is a performance driven industry. Highly successful people don't only perform very well, they also perform often.

---

*The single best investment one
can make is in one's self.*
Marco-ism

To you, dear reader, I end with this. If you think this book has helped you because you've read it, I'm sorry to tell you that it hasn't. Not yet. You don't get paid for what you know; you get paid for what you do. My question to you is, what are you going to do now?

I urge you to go over the action steps in this book and write down your answers. Stay competitive with yourself against your goals. Create the new habits you have learned in this book. Wake up earlier, read, prepare, get into meaningful conversations – not sales conversations, close with conviction, invest in you, and help others.

Life doesn't have to be hard. Making six figures doesn't have to be hard. If you use your time wisely, it's actually easy. Too Easy.

Notes

MARCO-ISMS

Chapter 1

- Belief is the most powerful motivator known to mankind
- Plan B is a dream killer
- You'll never benefit from what you know, you'll benefit from what you do

Chapter 2

- Focus more on what happens because of you instead of what happens to you
- Take criticism seriously, not personally

Chapter 3

- Don't love money. Love what money allows you to do

Chapter 4

- Your text will be answered more than your voicemail
- Nothing worth having comes without sacrifice

Chapter 5

- No one likes to work with selfish people

Chapter 6

- The more people you help, the more income you earn

- It's your obligation to each prospect to use every ethical method to speak to them

Chapter 7

- Price is almost never the issue
- Price is not a big deal unless you make it one
- "It's too expensive" is better than "I'm not interested"

Chapter 8

- Don't bash your competition. Ever.

Chapter 9

- Soft closers are sheep, and sheep get led
- You never have the right to be a hard closing jerk
- Numbers on the board mean nothing unless it's paid business

Chapter 10

- It's much easier to get referrals than new business
- We can't help broke people

Chapter 11

- Beasts run through obstacles and devour whatever stands in its way
- How can you lose a sale you never had?

Chapter 12

- I'm working to leave a legacy while I'm alive – Marco-ism
- There's plenty of money for everybody – Marco-ism
- The single best investment one can make is in one's self.

Acknowledgments:

To my father Guillermo Figueroa, you taught and showed me what it was to be disciplined and how valuable a strong work ethic is. You led from the front and always provided our family with what we needed and loved us in your own special way.

To my sister Dorothy Kolody, you were always supportive of me when I was younger all while putting up with my selfishness and immaturity at times. You are a great role model for sisters and moms everywhere.

And to my mother Cynthia Ann Figueroa, the most loving and courageous person I have ever known. Always filled with life and happiness, you helped shaped my personality of who I am today. I think of you always and miss you dearly every day.

About the Author

Marcos Figueroa was born in Trenton, Michigan. He grew up rooting for the Detroit Red Wings and Michigan Wolverines while living in the Detroit area for the first ten years of his life. He then moved with his parents to Brunswick, Ohio where he graduated high school before enlisting in the U.S. Army.

He began his career in 1991 as a Bradley Fighting Vehicle Mechanic stationed at Ft. Carson, Colorado. He served on active duty until 1995 then transitioned into the U.S. Army Reserve. He then entered the mortgage industry as a loan officer in 1997 then moved into sales leadership roles in 2000. In October of 2001, he was mobilized with the 88th MP Company out of Ft. Eustis, VA in support of post 9/11 operations and returned in June of 2002 where he then moved to the Tampa, FL area in 2002 where he was a branch sales manager for a well-respected mortgage lender.

After the market crash of 2008 Marcos looked for a new career where he could further utilize his talents. In 2009 he entered the health insurance industry and found himself in an organization where helping and serving others was first and foremost the primary objective.

He knew he found his calling. His passion for helping others clearly showed in his production numbers and was on track to move up in the standings until he once again had to put his civilian career on hold.

In March of 2013, Marcos received mobilization orders and was again deployed with his unit in support of Operation Enduring Freedom serving in the role of Military Police at Camp Sabalu-Harrison in Parwan Province, Afghanistan. He returned in 2014 and is currently assigned to the 317th MP BN out of Tampa, FL.

Marcos immediately picked up where he left off but this time with a new sense of appreciation for the opportunity before him. Over the last several years he has proven himself as a top personal producer and has led his field sales force to earn recognition as the top team in the country within his organization.

When Marcos is not working, he enjoys spending time with his wife Migdalia Figueroa (Dali) whom he married in 2018. They enjoy spending time traveling throughout the U.S. and abroad. He takes advantage of what the Tampa Bay area has to offer with its wide variety of restaurants, Broadway shows, professional sporting venues, and waterways.

Marcos is a speaker, trainer, mentor, and coach to many high-achieving sales professionals.

Contact Marcos for speaking or training engagements

via **Marcos.figueroa@ushadvisors.com**

CPSIA information can be obtained
at www.ICGtesting.com
Printed in the USA
FSHW021405170319
56319FS

9 780998 699233